Kindest Regards
your help was most appreciated
Hugh Dan

THE BEN RACE

- the supreme test of athletic fitness

Hugh Dan MacLennan

Ben Nevis Race Association

December 1994

Printed by Highland Printers

Design, origination and layout by Hiscan Ltd,
Inverness, Scotland

Published by Ben Race Association, Fort William

British Library in Publication Data:

A catalogue record for this book is obtainable from
the British Library

ISBN 0 952 4453 2 8

The Red Burn - nearly half-way.

A. Gillespie

Anail a'Ghàidheil am mullach: The Gael takes his breath at the top. Runners in the 1994 Race.
Rob Howard

Introduction

Oh! for a sight of Ben Nevis!
Methinks I see him now,
As the morning sunlight crimsons
The snow-wreath on his brow.
As he shakes away the shadows,
His heart the sunshine thrills,
And he towers high and majestic,
Amidst a thousand hills.

(Mary MacKellar 1834-1890)

The relationship between man and his environment is on the one hand an understandable thing, on the other, a matter which defies belief. So it is with Ben Nevis. It is well known of course, that people have made it to the top at a more leisurely pace and for a wide variety of reasons, for much longer. But this volume confines itself to the history of the Ben Nevis race over the last 100 years - the supreme test of athletic fitness.

I was born and brought up in the shadow of Ben Nevis. Until September 27, 1994 - 99 years to the day the William Swan made his famous ascent which started the whole proceedings which form the basis of this volume - I had never been to the top. Having achieved that feat - stood on the highest point in Britain, on top of arguably the most dangerous mountain in Europe - I believe I can understand why men and women have wanted to run to the top in the shortest possible time for the last 100 years.

As I set out on my first ascent on that beautiful day in September, I had little real understanding of what lay before me; for all that the aching steps I eventually took seemed to be couched in a painful familiarity, won from the fascinating accounts of triumphs and failures I had read as I researched the history of the race.

Making the ascent of Ben Nevis, in whatever form and at whatever pace, is simply and unforgettable experience. By way of the path there are the land-marks - Clint's Rock, the aluminium bridges and the Red Burn, with the ever present "familiar squat cairns" dotted around, silently acknowledging the frailty of human nature in its many wierd and wonderful forms.

And as the chain saws cry in the distance and jets scream past underneath with a stunning disregard for the majesty of the surroundings, there are also the poignant moments which only the athletic challenge and the solitude of the mountains can bring. The somtimes eerie silence and stillness of a perfect day with only the gentlest breeze tugging at the beautifully selected flowers in a family wreath - *"To Len with love"*.

Far beyond, there is the summit which can only be described as an unforgettable place. Its cairns and its crosses, its buildings and its panoramic view, the encroaching chill and the thrill of potential danger in the gaping jaws of the gullies just feet away. There is simply no place on earth like it. And I can only assume that I saw it at its best, in near perfect conditions, on an exceptionally clear day in September.

The hundreds of runners who have reached the summmit as part of the sporting challenge which this book outlines will rarely have had time to admire the view. Getting to the top and back down again in the shortest possible time is always their aim. Getting to the top back down again in one piece was mine. In much the same way as the people of Paris rarely go to the top of the Eiffel Tower and the people of London tend not to visit the Tower of London, so I had admired Ben Nevis from a distance for 38 years. It will always be one of my greatest regrets that I never took part in a Ben Nevis Race. As a small boy clutching my first ever gold-fish, won at the Race in the King George V Park, I gazed in awe as the mud-spattered heroes struggled to the line as the lightening crashed around us. It always seemed to be wet on Ben Race days !

But having drawn this volume together and achieved the summit, I feel as if I have been part of the Ben Race for ever. I feel I know what made William Swan set out on his bicycle that fateful September day in 1895, and what keeps Eddie Campbell driving to the top even now, after many hundreds of ascents.

The men and women who appear in the following pages are all heroes. Their achievements cannot be over-stated. They are true sportsmen and women and they have all contributed over the years into making the Ben Nevis Race the supreme test of athletic fitness.

Hugh Dan MacLennan
North Kessock,
September, 1994

The second of the 1903 races - Ewen MacKenzie, Hugh Kennedy and R. Dobson of Maryhill at the start.   *The Herald*

The early view of runners from Banavie - across Lochy Bridge. An American, impressed with the sight, is reported to have asked: "Say, guy, is it whisky that's in these pipes?"

Acknowledgments

I am in the first instance indebted to the Ben Nevis Race Association for their invitation to undertake this challenge which was in its own way something of a mountain. I would like to place on record my thanks in particular to Alister MacIntyre the Chairman, who has been most supportive of the project from the outset; the indefatigable George MacFarlane who, as Secretary of the BNRA, carries a great burden of the responsibility for the organisation of the event, and his brother Sandy; also Treasurer Rob Bowie for his assistance, guidance and support in matters pecuniary.

I am particularly indebted to a number of individuals who have contributed greatly to the history of the great institution which is the Ben Nevis Race. Their help in the production of this history has been invaluable: Kathleen MacPherson (Connochie), Terry Confield of Lochaber Mountain Rescue Team, Brian Kearney, Charlie Fitzimmons, and other runners and members of the Committee too numerous to mention individually.

A number of people have assisted with the production of this volume by allowing me access to their personal collections and archives: Neil Clark, Fort William; Mrs Donald MacDonald, Fort William; Ronnie Campbell, Fort William; J. Dunlevy, Caol; Donnie A. Fraser, Inverness; James MacIntyre, Inverness; Hugh MacLeod, Maryburgh.

It is no disrespect to those already named if I single out the contribution of Ian Abernethy of the West Highland News Agency whose cuttings' files and personal store of Lochaber lore were invaluable and Anthony MacMillan whose research in terms of photographic material gleaned by his late father Alistair was invaluable. It is with great sadness that I learned of "Scoop's" passing just days before the 1994 Race. In many ways the fruits of his labours on the pages of this volume are the most eloquent tribute I can pay to his efforts on behalf of athletics in Lochaber.

This book would obviously not be what it is without the magnificent contribution of several photographers who have helped enormously: Ewen Weatherspoon, Inverness, John Paul, Inverness, Alex Gillespie and Jimmy Murdoch, Fort William, Coll MacDougall, Oban and Anthony and Alistair MacMillan of the West Highland News Agency without whose help this book would most certainly not have been possible. Specific thanks are due to John Paul and Duncan McEwen (insert) for their contribution to the cover photography, and to Hugh Barron and George MacFarlane for their assistance with proofing. My thanks also to the staff of Hiscan - particularly Stephen Connor and Aileen Snody for their diligence and above all, patience and understanding.

My sincere thanks to J. Baines, Earnest Press, Anglesey for permission to use material from his superb reprint of W. T. Kilgour's classic work *Twenty years on Ben Nevis*. the NCC through Scottish Natural Heritage for permission to reproduce material from *Ben Nevis and Glen Nevis*; Carol Kyros Walker and her publishers AUP for permission to reproduce material from her volume *Walking with Keats*; likewise Ken Crocket for his assistance, largely through to the pages of the splendid *Ben Nevis*.

I also owe a great debt to the Editors of *the Oban Times* and *Inverness Courier* in particular for permission to quote freely from their priceless archives; the Editor of the Scots Magazine and Peoples Journal for other material used and also staff at *The Herald*, principally Bob Jeffrey, Managing Editor; Eddie Rodger, Sports Editor and Ian Watson and his staff in the Picture Library.

The staff of Inverness Library are to be thanked for their unfailing courtesy and attention, particularly those in the Reference section and I am greatly in the debt of Fiona Marwick, Curator of the West Highland Museum in Fort William for her assistance at various points.

Finally, I owe a huge debt to Coll MacDougall of Oban whose tireless efforts plundering the archives of that marvellous store of West Highland history which is *The Oban Times*, enabled me to devote time to other aspects of this project which might not have been available. Coll's heroic effort has been the single most important contribution to the (I hope) success of this account of similarly heroic endeavour.

I should also thank my wife Kathleen for her assistance, consideration and understanding, particularly when it must have appeared that she had been deserted for my Apple Mac when deadlines loomed larger than normal.

The list is almost endless, and I must apologise to anyone missed out. No contribution was too little; all were gratefully received and I trust I have done justice to the efforts and contributions of those named above have been done justice in the following pages.

I am, of course, solely responsible for any of the shortcomings which may be discovered.

Hugh Dan MacLennan
North Kessock
September, 1994

The following made major contributions to the production either in kind or through financial contributions:

HRC

Lochaber District Council

ScotRail

The Herald

The Scottish Collection

The following made three-figure financial contributions:

Arjo Wiggins

Bank of Scotland

Ben Nevis Distillery

BSW Sawmills (Kilmallie)

Coll MacDougall

Glen Nevis Holdiays

Inverness Insurance Centre

Kelly Associates

Mrs Rena Smith, Ben View Guest House

MacFarlane's Chemist   MacFARLANE & SON

Milton Hotels

Nevis Bank Hotel

Royal Bank of Scotland   The Royal Bank of Scotland plc

The Oban Times   The Oban Times

Scotia Timber & Building Supplies

Alex Gillesie Photography

Other financial contributions were made by:

Alcan

Marine Harvest

Nevisport Ltd

To the winner, the spoils.
The 1994 winner Ian Holmes with cousins Gavin and Jonathan Bland (left, 2nd and 3rd respectively).

Ben Nevis, from Corpach

On Ben Nevis: A Memory

My heart the beauties of the night enthral,
A dream of tenderness and pure delight;
Round me below the fog-lakes slowly fall,
Yet linger in the valleys, pure and white.

Calmly the moon in her pale splendour shines,
And casts o'er all her opalescent shroud;
Mountain and hill stand forth in softest lines,
Peeping like myriad islands through the cloud.

Blest is my soul to know this tranquil hour,
Earth with its sin and strife is far away;
Love seems the essence of the eternal power,
Life is no riddle but a harmony.

John S. Begg, 1897

Foreword

It was in the Spring of 1951 that the late George MacPherson and I were approached by the Town Clerk Bob Dow, asking us if we would consider organising a Ben Nevis Race in the autumn. He told us that the race had not been run since 1944, but that Provost George MacFarlane was prepared to present the trophy which had originally been put forward in 1937.

George MacPherson and I obtained the help of our dear friend Duncan MacIntyre (the 1943 Race winner) and we three formed the Ben Nevis Race Committee, later to become the Ben Nevis Race Association. Our committee room was provided through the courtesy of Kenny Nicholson in a "certain room" in the Alexandra Hotel and that is where our plans were laid.

It struck me at the time, having lived in Fort William from 1947 to 1957, that we were in possession of something that no other place in Great Britain owned - THE HIGHEST MOUNTAIN - and I had a vision of athletes from all over the British Isles being attracted to Fort William for the race, provided it could be well and safely organised and properly marketed. Bad weather would be no obstacle to the type of athlete I knew we would attract. As Mr Donald Duff wrote in the foreword to my own book, "the test was of all-round physiological fitness under conditions unobtainable elsewhere." And we had a dedicated nucleus of local competitors, Eddie Campbell, the Kearney brothers, the Petries, Jimmy Conn and others who later formed the Lochaber Athletic Club which dominated the race in those early years. Incidentally the tankard with which the club presented me on my departure from Fort William is still being put to good use!

I was serving with the Lovat Scouts (T.A.) at the time and my signal detachment used the Ben Race as a training exercise, and for many years Lovat Scout signallers faithfully carried their No. 9 sets (and batteries) to the summit, assisting in the safety of the runners and providing information to the commentator in King George V Park.

I must pay tribute to my colleague at the Ben Nevis Distillery, William D. MacKenzie for the help he provided year after year circularising athletic clubs all over Britain and collating entry forms etc. I must also mention the R.A.F. Mountain Rescue teams, especially the fortitude and dedication shown by a certain detachment on a wet and miserable day and night in 1957.

A word of acknowledgement also to Olympic Gold Medallist Chris Brasher and Olympian John Disley, who by their presence gave special credence to the Race. It was Lady Hermione of Lochiel who gave me the Cup now being awarded annually to the best over-forty runner. She had originally been presented with this cup when she was a little girl at an annual horticultural show in her home in Brodick, Arran.

Many, many people have contributed to the success of the Ben Nevis Race. The *esprit de corps* of the citizens of Fort William transformed a race of 21 competitors in 1951 to over 500 in 1985, and I am proud to have played a small role in the Ben Race saga.

I am also honoured indeed to have been asked to contribute the foreword to this book. I wish the Ben Nevis Race Association every success with it and look forward to meeting my many friends in Fort William and from far afield, God willing, at the Ben Nevis Race centenary in Fort William in 1995.

Charles W S Steel
Ontario
Canada
September, 1994

Contents

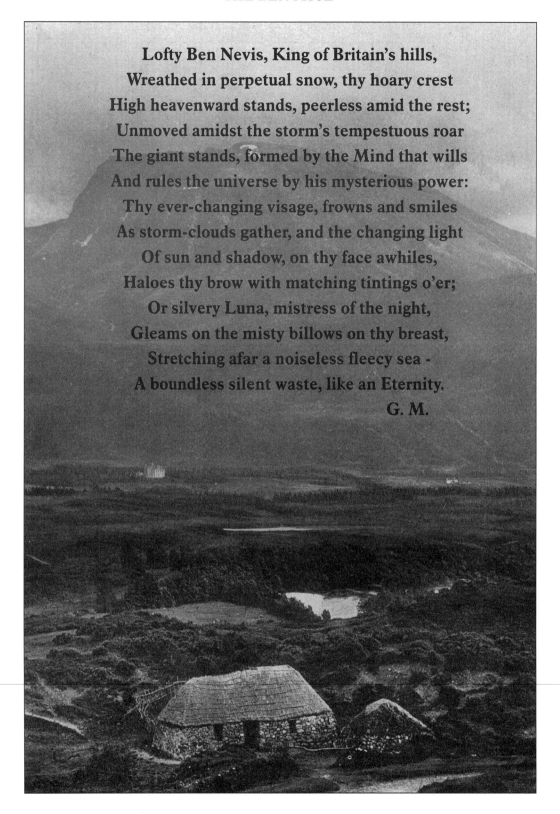

Lofty Ben Nevis, King of Britain's hills,
Wreathed in perpetual snow, thy hoary crest
High heavenward stands, peerless amid the rest;
Unmoved amidst the storm's tempestuous roar
The giant stands, formed by the Mind that wills
And rules the universe by his mysterious power:
Thy ever-changing visage, frowns and smiles
As storm-clouds gather, and the changing light
Of sun and shadow, on thy face awhiles,
Haloes thy brow with matching tintings o'er;
Or silvery Luna, mistress of the night,
Gleams on the misty billows on thy breast,
Stretching afar a noiseless fleecy sea -
A boundless silent waste, like an Eternity.

G. M.

Chapter 1

The Ben Race:
the supreme test of athletic stamina

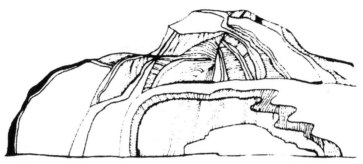

Celebrating 100 years of running on Ben Nevis

Ben Nevis, highest mountain of the British Isles, in the district of Lochaber, Highland Region (until 1975 in the county of Inverness), Scotland. Its summit, reaching 4,406 ft (1,343m), is a plateau of about 100ac (40ha), with a slight slope to the south and a sheer face to the Northeast. Snow lies in some parts all year, and permafrost conditions (i.e. the presence of a permanently frozen soil layer) are almost reached. The mountain consists of a superstructure of volcanic rocks surmounting the ancient schists, with granites intruded of the Scottish Highlands. On the summit are ruins of an abandoned hotel and a former meteorological station, access to which was provided by a bridle path, nowhere steeper than a gradient of one in five, from Glen Nevis at Achintee.

56° 48' N, 5° 00' W

The description offered by Encyclopaedia Britannica of arguably one of the most ferocious mountains in Europe is of necessity brief and to the point. Its very brevity, however, disguises the many intriguing facets of Britain's grandest mountain mass - its beauty and majesty, ferocity, fickleness and mystery. These are the very qualities which have intrigued and defied travellers, climbers, scientists and runners for centuries, much longer in fact than the wonderful efforts of the last one hundred years commemorated in this volume.

Ben Nevis attracts many visitors simply because, at 1344 metres (4406 feet), it is the highest mountain in the British Isles. However, it would surely justify great attention even if the altitude of its summit were not supreme, for it is by any stretch of the imagination, a magnificent mountain with a varied and complex form. Its base, which rises from only a little above sea level, is also bordered to the south and west by one of the most beautiful glens in Scotland - Glen Nevis.

Glen Nevis

It would require a person with a fecund imagination to concoct mentally a scene more entrancing or impressive than the prospect from Ben Nevis in the glorious days of summer. Lakes and streams innumerable, rolling moorland wastes, rivers, copse, corry, and tarn, flit before the vision, and vie with each other for predominance. Now and then, mayhap, a thick bank of cloud gathers in the surrounding valleys, leaving only the hill-tops visible, and immediately a transformation of the scene occurs. To all appearance, one is gazing on a wide expanse of ocean studded with countless islets, some of which, as the film rises, gradually disappear, as if buffeted and over-washed by surf. In closer proximity are yawning chasms and steep declivities, the eternal snow ridges contrasting strongly with the dark basaltic rock forming the angles and the precipes, while the prolixity of colours, the murmur of the breeze, and the sublimity and peace of all around, speak to the heart as nothing in the lower world can.

(Kilgour, *Twenty Years*, p.90)

The origin of the word Nevis is obscure. The name is applied not only to the mountain, and its bordering river and glen, but also to a large sea loch in the district of Knoydart some 40 kilometres (25 miles) to the west. The Gaelic form of the mountain's name Beinn Nimheis, has been linked with various Gaelic and Irish words including 'neamhaise' meaning terrible, 'neimheil' meaning poisonous and 'neamh' meaning a raw and bitingly keen atmosphere. Most of the suggested meanings imply a dreadful character.

'The river Nevis of Glen Nevis at the foot of Ben Nevis is *Abhainn Nimhe*is or *Nibheis - mh* can hardly be distinguished from *bh* in pronunciation after n, which makes the syllable nasal in any case. The name recurs in Loch Nevis on the west coast of Inverness-shire. A third instance, which may or may not be of the same origin, is Knocknevis in Minigaff Parish, with a small brook from it to the Dee. In poetry we have *tar èis leoghuin Loch Nimheis*, 'after (the death of) the lion of Loch Nevis,' in a bardic poem, c. 1705. A poem by Iain Lom mentions *Sròn Neamhais*, 'point of Nevis' (the river), but the rime shows that the poet pronounced it *Sròn Nimheis*; so also in his poem on Inverlochy he makes Nimheis rime with pillein. Adopting the spelling Nibheis, Macbain took the name from an early Nebestis or Nebesta, 'the root *neb* or *nebh* is connected with clouds and water, and gives us the classical idea of Nymph, root *nbh* .... There was a river in ancient Spain called the Nebis, now Neyva, which may also show the same root.' This is probably going too far afield. If we take the spelling *Nimheis* the name may be compared with the Irish river-name *Nem, Neim (Neimh)*, gen. *Neme*, one of the thirteen 'royal rivers'. This name is formally identified with O. Ir. *nem, neim*, venom. gen. *Neme*, and probably means 'venemous one', the opposite of our *Fine. Nimheis* (genitive), Nevis appears to be the same with addition of a suffix: nom. *Nemess*, later Neimheas, gen. *Nimheis*; this would become *Nimheas, Nimheis* in Sc. Gaelic, as *neimh*, venom, becomes nimh. This explains also the anglicized form Nevis, which dates from a time before *Neimheas* became *Nimheas*. A sixteenth century bard says of Glen Nevis :-

'Gleann Nibheis, gleann na gcloch,
Gleann am bi an gart anmoch;
Gleann fada fiadhaich, fàs,
Sluagh bradach an mhìoghnàis.'

'Glen Nevis, glen of stones, a glen where
corn ripens late; a long, wild, waste glen,
with thievish folk of evil habit.'

Another version has :-

Gleann ris d'chuir Dia a chùl;
Amar sgùrainn an domhain mhòir,'

'A great glen on which God has turned his
back; the slop-pail of the great world.'

(W.J.Watson, *Celtic Place-names of Scotland*, pp 471-472)

Ben Nevis from Corpach c. 1830.

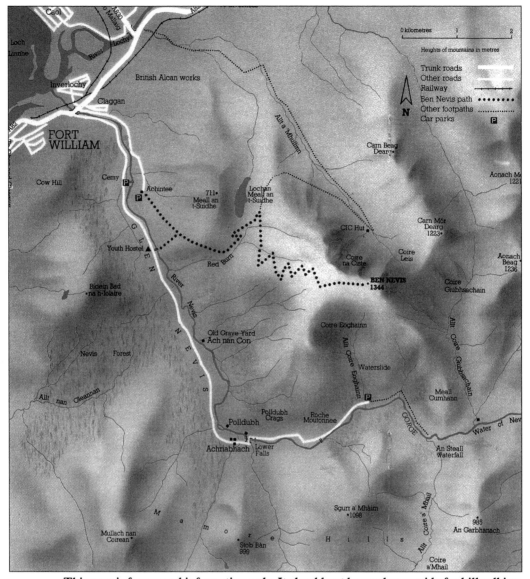

This map is for general information only. It should not be used as a guide for hillwalking.

The best time of year to attempt this route is probably in August, by which time the plateau is normally free of snow. Even then it is essential to wear proper clothing - including a full set of wind and waterproof outer garments should also be taken. It is recommended that some six hours be allowed for a comfortable ascent and descent.

The following advice is offered by Lochaber Mountain Rescue Team:

1. **Allow plenty of time for the trip**. The average non-mountaineer would be around four hours for the ascent and three for the descent. Remember that your party should move at the speed of the slowest member and it is unwise to split up. Children must not be allowed to go up alone nor must they be allowed to go on ahead as it is very easy to get lost on this mountain.

2. **Get a good map of the 'Ben'**. The 1:25,000 Mountaineer map of Ben Nevis is recommended. Stick to the zig-zags and don't be tempted to take short cuts as there are many dangerous descent routes which should be avoided. In bad weather, the return route from the summit plateau can be difficult to find. The only sure way is to have a map and a compass.

3. **Remember that even in Summer there can be snow on the path, and the weather can turn Arctic like in a very short time**, so waterproof/windproof jacket and over trousers are essential. Get a mountain weather forecast before you set out or check displays in local outdoor shops. If in doubt, don't go.

4. **Wear stout footwear**. Fashion shoes and boots are definitely not suitable, neither are sandals. Take plenty of food for the trip.

5. **If you feel unwell or the weather turns nasty, turn back**. You can always try on another day.

6. **The views from the summit are magnificent and make it well worth while, but please don't spoil it for others**. Take your rubbish back with you and please do not throw rubbish or stones over the cliffs as someone may be climbing up.

The main accidents to tourists are:-

1. Taking short cuts onto very steep ground and falling, resulting in head injuries, broken limbs and sometimes fatalities.

2. Taking short cuts and getting lost.

3. Getting lost in inclement weather.

4. Getting separated from the main party.

5. Cardiac arrest usually brought on by trying to keep up with fitter members of the party.

The Scottish Collection   *Andrew McKenna*

Both the mountain and the glen are outstanding for their scenery and natural history.

The West Highlands is one of the wettest areas in Britain. The average annual rainfall in Fort William is two metres, but this figure increases to more than four metres on the summit of Ben Nevis, where much of the precipitation falls as snow. At sea level the climate is relatively mild and equable due to the influence of the Gulf Stream, but conditions become increasingly severe with altitude. Snow lies on the summit of Ben Nevis for much of the year and it rarely disappears altogether from the gullies on the shadowy north-east face.

Measurements at the former observatory on the summit (which functioned from 1883 to 1904) indicated a mean annual temperature just below freezing point, and an average of 261 gales per year with wind speeds greater than 80 kilometres per hour (50 miles per hour). The temperature on the summit is generally 9 degrees Celsius colder than at the base of the mountain, and it can be calm in Glen Nevis when there is a gale blowing on the plateau. So although the footpath up the north-western flank of Ben Nevis is often referred to as the "Tourist Route", its ascent should never be undertaken lightly.

Ben Nevis

The Ben Nevis massif, in common with most of the Highlands of Scotland, is built of rocks representing the eroded root of the ancient Caledonian Mountain Chain. This chain once extended from Scandinavia across the northern part of Britain to the eastern side of North America. At one time it must have been similar to the present day Andean chain of South America, but it was worn down by erosion long ago and subsequently fragmented by the drifting apart of North America, Greenland, and Europe.

The Caledonian mountains began to form some 500 million years ago when two huge 'plates' in the earth's crust collided with each other. A thick sequence of marine sediments became deformed by the great pressure and heat associated with this mountain building episode, and thereby turned into metamorphic (or 'changed') rocks. Siltstones were changed to schists, mudstones were changed to slates, limestones were changed to marbles, and quartz sandstones changed to quartzite.

Great pressure also caused the rock layers to become overturned in gigantic flat lying folds called 'nappes'. In many instances these folds were themselves subsequently refolded. Sufficient heat was generated in the base of the mountain chain to cause rocks to melt. Large volumes of molten rock or 'magma' were formed within the earth's crust, and in places this escaped to the surface and erupted as lava. At times the magma erupted from long deep fissures which resulted in the formation of features called dykes.

Huge chambers of magma which cooled slowly in the earth's crust eventually crystallised to form large masses of granite. Many granites exposed today in the Highlands of Scotland, including Ben Nevis granite, were formed about 400 million years ago during the final stages of the Caledonian mountain building episode. Heat given out by the magma chambers passed into and baked the surrounding 'country rock'. This caused new minerals to develop in the metamorphic rocks around the margin of the Ben Nevis granite.

The Great Glen Fault became active shortly after the formation of the Ben Nevis granite. Large scale movement took place along this fault, as a consequence of which the rocks lying north-west of the Great Glen and Loch Linnhe slid horizontally many tens of thousands of kilometres relative to the remainder of Scotland.

Ben Nevis

The final phase in the shaping of Ben Nevis and Glen Nevis took place during the last two million years when vast ice sheets built up in northern latitudes around the world. On several occasions the northern part of Britain was completely covered by ice. At times of less extensive ice cover the highest summits remained exposed and glaciers gouged out corries on the sides of mountains and deepened the valleys to form U-shaped glens. Side valleys which held smaller quantities of ice were not eroded as deeply and so formed what are known as 'hanging valleys' - for example, the glen of the Allt a'Mhuilinn, which lies immediately north-east of Ben Nevis, 'hangs' above the Great Glen.

As the ice retreated at the close of the last glaciation about 10,000 years ago, the scene was set for the return of plant life. At first the climate was harsh, and the plants were similar - even at sea level - to those found today in the Arctic or the high Alps.

During the succeeding thousands of years, the climate improved and gradually the more warmth-loving species spread northwards. The first tree to arrive was the birch, followed by the Scots pine, then the alder, willow, hazel and oak. This warming reached its peak around 7,000 years ago, and the extent of woodland cover in the Highlands was greater then than at any time since. At the same time, the Arctic-Alpine species retreated to higher altitudes where the conditions were more severe.

After this the climate became cooler and wetter, and extensive development of peat began to take place. Many of the pine stumps found preserved in high-altitude peat bogs in the Highlands (such as those in upper Glen Nevis) date from this phase. Many are more than 5,000 years old.

The exact date of man's arrival in the Highlands is not known, but evidence found on the Isle of Rhum National Nature Reserve indicates that settlements existed there in the Mesolithic, or Middle Stone Age, about 8,500 years ago. However, man did not begin to modify the environment significantly until farming methods were introduced in the Neolithic, or New Stone Age, about 6,000 years ago. Some of the earliest metal implements to have been found in Scotland were discovered just north of Ben Nevis by the bank of the River Lochy in the early 1980s. They are believed to date back to the Bronze Age some 4,000 years ago.

Only the lower part of Glen Nevis is permanently settled at the present day, although human influence extends right to the top of Ben Nevis. A variety of land uses occur which affect the composition of the area's plant and animal communities. The outlines of old 'lazy beds' (narrow strips of cultivated land) can be seen in the floor of Glen Nevis on the east bank of the river just over a kilometre upstream from the Youth Hostel.

However, the main farming activity in the glen nowadays involves sheep and a lesser number of cattle. Sheep of the Scottish blackface and Cheviot breeds graze extensively over the hills for most of the year. They are much more selective grazers than cattle, and by choosing the more palatable fine-leaved grasses can encourage the spread of coarser, more tussocky vegetation. In winter they browse on twiggy growth, such as bog myrtle and young tree seedlings. This suppresses shrub growth and prevents the regeneration of woodland.

For the last 200 years, since sheep began to outnumber cattle in the west Highlands, it has been the tradition to burn hill vegetation, usually in the spring to encourage young growth. This process provides an 'early bite' of grass for sheep, but also kills young trees, and if done too frequently promotes the growth of grasses at the expense of shrubs such as heather.

> **The sides of Ben Nevis mountains descend in broad, smooth, grassy declivities, some of which are elegantly dotted with natural wood. The heights on the other side spread out in wide marshy flats; while the intermediate ground gradually offers a more expansive and appropriate field for the spade and the plough. First you have the sheep department of the farm at Auchandaul, a very extensive tract; and next there is the large farm of Leanachan, which, with the exception of a few fields in the neighbourhood of the dwelling-house, is devoted exclusively to pasture. The solitary and deserted appearance of these sheep-walks strikes a stranger at once. No human being is seen as you stretch your eye along the strath. The very sheep, at this season of the year, hide themselves on the tops of the hills. No dikes, or fences, or any other trace of labour, announce to you that man has been here. No living voice, or hum of industry, is heard; as the listening ear catches the distant plash of the mountain torrent, or the dreary rustle of the wind as it sweeps over the long grass, a feeling is awakened akin to that experienced by eastern travellers when standing amidst the solitude of some fallen Babylon, or some deserted Shinar, stricken by the curse of God. An old Highlandman, who has frequently topped Ben Nevis and his numerous satellites, pointed out to me, without moving a foot, the spots where, in his day, stood six hamlets, each containing ten or twelve families. Scarcely a stone of the cottages are left; and, except for the small circular gardens, which are still preserved to the eye by the remains of their feal enclosures, it would be impossible to discover the slightest trace of these homes of former generations.**
>
> **(R. Somers, *Letters from the Highlands*, 1846)**

Red deer seek out high ground in summer, but tend to avoid places with numerous human visitors such as Ben Nevis. They can often be seen in the quieter section of the glen above the Nevis Gorge, particularly over the winter months when large herds gather on lower ground. The stags and hinds live separately for most of the year and only associate during the mating season (or 'rut') in October.

GLEN NEVIS *The Scottish Collection*   *A. Gillespie*

Much of the western side of lower Glen Nevis is given over to forestry plantations. These are of coniferous species not native to Britain, including Norway and
sitka spruce, lodgepole pine and silver fir. Other planted trees in the lower glen
include the fine specimens of beech, and sycamore around Glen Nevis House, and
on the old graveyard at Ach nan Con.

Thousands of people visit Ben Nevis and Glen Nevis every year for various forms
of recreation, including picnicking, sightseeing, nature watching, pony trekking, hill
walking, hill running, rock climbing and ice climbing. Many of them reach the summit of Ben Nevis by one route or another. The variety of geological features, and the
range of plant and animal communities found on Ben Nevis are so important in
national terms that the whole of Ben Nevis, and most of Glen Nevis is included in a
large Site of Special Scientific Interest (SSSI). This designation allows Scottish
Natural Heritage (SNH), the government agency charged with the responsibility of
looking after the natural environment to advise and assist landowners in managing
the site so that its outstanding natural features can be maintained, and wherever
appropriate enhanced.

Glen Nevis is one of the finest and most spectacular glens in Scotland, and is a
splendid example of a glacially deepened valley. At the top car park, some 10 kilometres from the entrance to the glen, the floor of the glen is still less than 150 metres
above sea level. Many features of interest can be examined in Glen Nevis without the
need for hill walking.

Ben Nevis. Note the pipeline centre left leading to the aluminium works.

In 1924 work began on a remarkable hydro-electric scheme that is still being used today to generate power for British Alcan's Lochaber Smelter at Fort William. Its construction was a major feat of engineering and involved driving a 4.6 metre diameter tunnel for 24 kilometres (15 miles) from Loch Treig to Fort William through the northern flank of the Ben Nevis range. All the major streams draining from the north side of the Ben Nevis range feed into the scheme. To further increase the capacity of the system the Laggan dam was constructed across the River Spean and the water from Laggan reservoir now drains by tunnel into Loch Treig.

The main tunnel from Loch Treig ends in a massive surge shaft over 70 metres deep on the northern flank of Meall an t-Suidhe. From the bottom of the shaft water is channelled into five pipes (clearly visible on the hillside) and flows into the power house in the British Alcan works. More than 100,000 kilograms of aluminium are produced there each day.

Inverlochy Castle.

"The sublimity of prospect, the variety of phenomena, the rolling mists, and the raging tempests, have their own peculiar interest, and nonetheless enthralling is the study of gales and cloud effects, the torrential rains, the accumulation of snow, and the remarkable range and fluctuation of temperature; but the feature which probably most impresses the uninitiated is the stillness - the awful solitude - which at times prevails amid these vastnesses."

(W.T. Kilgour)

It is safe to assume that people have climbed Ben Nevis, or more accurately made the effort to get to the top, for as long as there has been a settlement at the head of Loch Linnhe. St Columba may even have given its majestic features a sideways glance as he headed up the Great Glen after he arrived in Scotland in 563AD.

Ben Nevis first appears on a map published by Blaeu of Amsterdam in 1654 - a Scottish edition of work based on the first topographical study of the country made by Timothy Pont (1565-1614). The mountain is there named "Bion Novesh" and one of the next references is to "Beniviss" in John Drummond of Balhaldy's *Memoirs of Locheill*:

> **"behind the fort there arises a huge mountain, of prodigious hight, called Beniviss, at that time adorned with a variety of trees and bushes, and now with a beautiful green. Its ascent is pretty steep, though smooth. The top or summit is plain, covered with perpetual snow, and darkened with thick clouds."**

This would seem to suggest that by the early 18th century mountain ascents were not exactly unheard of, but rare nonetheless. As time wore on, however, it is clear that the top of the highest point in the land began to hold no fears for many and was a most definite attraction.

Edward Burt in his *"Letters from a Gentleman in the North of Scotland"* published in 1754 tells how "Some English officers took it to their Fancy to go to the top, but could not attain it for Bogs and huge Perpendicular Rocks." Thomas Pennant, who toured Scotland in 1769 and 1772 also left a description, although he appears not to have attempted the ascent.

And there then followed a rash of visitors to the Ben, with the advent of the tourist in the latter half of the 18th century, as Ken Crocket details in his excellent *"Ben Nevis"*. They were soon followed by the scientists and the measurers from the Ordnance Survey.

Queen Victoria was also amongst the visitors.

> **"And now came the finest scene of all - Ben Nevis and its surrounding high hills, and others in the direction of Loch Laggan, all pink and glowing in that lovely afterglow (Alpengluhen) which you see in the Alps. It was glorious. It grew fainter and fainter till the hills became blue and then grey, and at last it became almost quite dark before we reached Banavie, and we only got home at a quarter past eight. As we drove out, I sketched Ben Nevis from the carriage."**

(*Queen Victoria's Highland Journals*, **Friday, September 12, 1873**)

Arguably the most famous visitor to make it to the top in this period (if we can believe him) was the poet John Keats who made a grand tour of Scotland with his friend Charles Brown, in 1818. That tour is fully documented in the superbly illustrated volume *Walking with Keats* by Carol Walker.

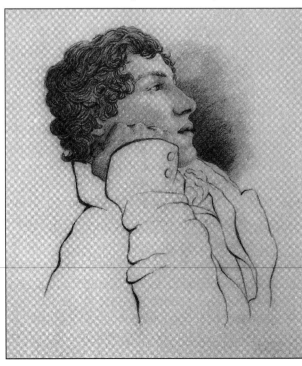

John Keats

In it, she details the ascent Keats allegedly made, recounting it in a four page letter to his brother Tom. The intriguing letter includes an imaginary dialogue between a Mrs Cameron and Ben Nevis. It runs to 74 lines. Mrs Cameron is said to have been the fattest woman of all Inverness-shire and had succeeded in climbing the Ben some years before our bard.

The Keats party set off at 5a.m. and soon faced the first of the climb *"after much fag and tug and a rest and a glass of whiskey apiece we gained the top of the first rise."*

The descent was clearly not to Keats' liking. *"It is almost like a fly crawling up a wainscot - Imagine the task of mounting 10*

St Paul's without the convenience of Stair cases. It was not so cold as I expected - yet cold enough for a glass of whiskey now and then." The descent too, he found laborious. "*I felt it horribly - 'Twas the most vile descent - shook me all to pieces.*"

In the letter to his brother, written from "Letter Findlay", there appears the following sonnet, said to have been composed at the top of Ben Nevis on Sunday, August 2, 1818:

> "Read me a Lesson, muse, and speak it loud
> Upon the top of Nevis blind in Mist!
> I look into the chasms and a shroud
> Vaprous doth hide them; just so much I wist
> Mankind do know of Hell: I look o'erhead
> And there is a sullen mist; even so much
> Mankind can tell of heaven: Mist is spread
> before the earth beneath me - even such
> Even so vague is Man's sight of himself.
> here are the craggy Stones beneath my feet;
> Thus much I know, that a poor witless elf
> I tread on them; that all my eye doth meet
> Is mist and crag - not only on this height,
> But in the world of thought and mental might."
>
> (Walker, *Walking North with Keats*, pp 208-209)

Above and below Ben Nevis Ascent
Walking North with Keats.

Keats' perambulations and the tourist boom which hit Scotland at the end of the 18th and 19th centuries were followed, and aided, by improved road networks, the Napoleonic Wars which re-directed people northwards, and as will be evident from the next chapter, the opening of the West Highland rail line.

Travelogues by the dozen followed, with each and every one expanding on the detail provided by the previous explorer. Gradually the scientists of the Scottish Meteorological Society took a more sophisticated and closer look at what was being found, and this eventually led to the building of a bridle path up the mountain, and the erection of an observatory on the summit which was manned continuously for 21 years.

From the beginning of June until October 14, 1881, the redoubtable Wragge made a daily ascent of the Ben, accompanied by his faithful Newfoundland dog Renzo.

THE OBSERVATORY AT BEN NEVIS: Mr. Wragge commenced work for and on behalf of the Society at the sea's level at five a.m. daily, using aneroid and sling thermometers, noting also the wind. Cloud observations are also taken at intervals at different altitudes during the descent of Ben Nevis working back to sea level, and also at the lake, both going and returning. The chief observations on the mountain are taken in three sets, viz. at 9.00, 9.30 and 10.00 a.m., Greenwich Time, and comprise, besides the instrumental readings, detailed observations on wind, cloud and prevailing conditions. Simultaneously, observations are taken by Mr. Colin Livingston at 9.00a.m. A new low level is shortly to be established, equipped chiefly by the Society. Already valuable results have been obtained on the Ben. On Tuesday morning the rigours of winter prevailed, and the thermometer box was frozen up, snow was falling briskly and the temperature four degrees below freezing point. The observations are understood to be merely preliminary to the establishment of a permanent Observatory on the mountain to the memory of David Hutcheson, who did so much towards opening up the resources of the West Highlands of Scotland.

(The Oban Times), **June 11, 1881**

A spectacular view of the hostile conditions under which the observers worked on Britain's highest mountain. The observatory was opened in October, 1883 and was closed down in 1904. The hotel, which was built of wood, continued for a short time after, but then it, too, was abandoned.

"Inclement rag" as he became known, was presented with a gold medal by the Society on March 22, 1882 for his heroic efforts the previous summer. He eventually went on to become Government Meteorologist in Queensland, Australia.

METEOROLOGY ON BEN NEVIS: The steamer service of David Hutcheson & Co., now continued by Mr. David MacBrayne, not only opened up and rendered familiar to us all, the most obscure and out -of-the-way nooks of the West, but it provided facilities and advantages to the teeming population of the city, which they were not slow to avail of and enjoy. The numerous friends of the genial and liberally minded organiser naturally determined that his memory should be kept green as a public benefactor, and they have chosen a national and novel mode of achieving their purpose. The erection of the Hutcheson Ben Nevis Observatory in which a staff of trained observers can constantly note the varying moments on the atmosphere, and aid in predicting its more serious disturbances, marks an era alike in Scottish meteorology and in popular ideas. It is a distinct evidence of scientific progress to find influential committee thus to seek to honour a popular favourite, and we can heartily congratulate them on this important movement that they have made in an effort to emancipate us from dependence for our weather predictions upon foreign enterprise and science. No more living mode of perpetuating a name could have been chosen than that of associating David Hutcheson with the first high level observatory, erected to provide daily knowledge of the atmosphere whose movements make and mar the fleets of the nations. (Glasgow News)

(*The Oban Times*, June 18, 1881)

Breakfast in the summit hotel c.1902.

The observatory, the work of which is detailed and beautifully illustrated in Ken Crocket's *"Ben Nevis"* and Kilgour's classic *"Twenty years"* published originally in 1905 was not, remarkably, the only attraction at the top of Ben Nevis. A small "hotel" was also built there - a small annex built by a Fort William hotelier after the building of the observatory. It was run by two local ladies who were, apparently, and understandably, frequently indignant at being awakened at all hours by visitors coming up to view the sunrise. Lunch was available for three shillings (15 pence), bed and breakfast for ten shillings (50 pence) and there were four small bedrooms.

Mrs Rodger and Sarah Cameron outside the Observatory Hotel.

BEN NEVIS: This king of mountains is now the great centre of attraction up here. Up to the beginning of June this year, Ben Nevis was simply the highest mountain in Great Britain, and as such was visited by many for the sake of getting perhaps the most extensive view in Great Britain, and no doubt on a clear fine day the view was worth all the trouble which one had in getting to the top. This year it had additional attractions which from a scientific point of view are well worthy of consideration, and the value of which are only beginning to be understood and appreciated. A full account of the meteorological instruments in use on Ben Nevis appeared in a recent issue of The TIMES; we need not, therefore, refer to them except in so far as it is necessary to our present object. The thermometer box is now enclosed in an iron cage for prohibition. The dimensions of the cage are four feet square by five foot six inches in length, and it was so constructed that it was carried to the summit in thirty-five loads. The above thing was carried up and erected in two days by Messrs. McCallum and Sons, builders, here, which considering the unfavourabliness of the weather, is highly creditable to them. The shelter hut put on the mountain was also built by Messrs. McCallum and Sons and is of the following dimensions - size of room inside: 11ft x 5ft and 6ft high at the sides. There is a fireplace and flue and the door is so built with respect to the fireplace that should the electric fluid pass in by the door it will escape by the flue and the observer's rest is placed at the farthest side to avoid danger. The walls are 3ft 6ins. thick at the base, tapering to 2ft 6ins. at the top. The roof is covered with strong sail canvas and prepared in the following way to make it wind and watertight: the canvas is first dipped in salt water, then painted with a composition made of Archangel tar and grease, and dried in four days. It was fixed on the roof by passing a cord through the eyelets made in the canvas and through holes made in a piece of wood fixed to the walls. The shelter as a temporary arrangement is a good one, but we hope that for the credit of our country that something more permanent in keeping with the importance of the place as a meteorological station that soon will be built up on top of the Ben. It is somewhat surprising that as yet there is no path or road made even to the tarn. Elsewhere in Scotland and England we find winding paths made to the top of less important mountains. How it comes to pass that a mountain which is a source of wealth to the district should be left as unattractive and inaccessible as possible to tourists.

(*The Oban Times*, **August 6, 1881**)

And predictably, perhaps, things soon started to go wrong:

ASCENT OF BEN NEVIS: The folly of ascending Ben Nevis without a guide has been demonstrated again. Three English ladies ascended the Ben on the 23rd inst., and when descending missed the path, and were only found the next morning at the top of a ravine on the west side of the Ben, by the Rev. Mr. MacColl and Peter MacDonald, a guide, who had gone in search of them. It was fortunate that they wandered to the west instead of the east side of the Ben, where there are precipices of a thousand feet.

(*The Oban Times*, **August 27, 1881**)

Ben Nevis: The summit from the air. *The Scottish Collection*   *A. Gillespie*

The three ladies were not at all pleased at a suggestion of their foolhardiness and gave an interview to the **DAILY TELEGRAPH** in which the following appears: "Finding a dry rock - a haven of refuge after the bogs we had gone through - we settled there for the night covered as well as we could in our plaids, and with our umbrellas overhead as a tent...."

(*The Oban Times*, September 10, 1881)

Soon travellers were arriving from far and wide aiming to reach the top.

Ascent of Ben Nevis : Mr. C. D. Cunningham of Edinburgh who has been staying at the Alexandra Hotel here, made the ascent of Ben Nevis on 3rd inst. He was accompanied by a guide. The ascent and descent was found to be a most difficult and dangerous thing owing to the sides of the Ben being coated with snow. But the view from the summit, the day being clear and fine, was magnificent.

(*The Oban Times*, January 13, 1883)

Ben Nevis: The view from the summit. *The Scottish Collection*   *Noel Williams*

ASCENT OF BEN NEVIS BY A LADY: Ben Nevis continues to be a great source of attraction here. Scarcely a day goes by without a large number ascending the Ben, very often as many as 30 or 40. On Thursday last, a Mr. and Mrs. A. T. Smith, from Kirkwall, accompanied by Colin Cameron, a guide, made the ascent and descent of the mountain in five hours and 45 minutes. This feat has not been performed in so short a time by a lady so far as is known, and yet Mrs. Smith did not seem to be much fatigued on her arrival in Fort William.

(*The Oban Times*, August 25, 1883)

THE BEN NEVIS OBSERVATORY : The highest section of the path to the summit of Ben Nevis was finished at noon on Thursday. The first pair of horses which ever ascended the Ben, made an ascent on Wednesday, carting two hundredweight of building material. The building of the permanent observatory, commenced on Wednesday. A number of horses are employed carrying material. The observatory will be finished within another month, should the good weather continue.

(*The Oban Times*, September 8, 1883)

William Kilgour, author, seated on the left with a party of visitors at the summit. He also operated a typing and shorthand business in Cameron Square.

The view one gets from the summit, when it is free from mist or when the atmosphere is clear, and the clouds lying lower, is indescribable. We have seen it when the summit is clear, and the cloud of fog lying far beneath, with only the peaks of the surrounding mountains, standing like islands in a boundless sea. We have watched the movements of the clouds, and noticed how they are attracted out of their course by the neighbouring hills and would then easier understand how and why the rain is so much oftener in the vicinity of the mountain ranges than in flat countries, where there is no attraction or break in the clouds. The fatigue of ascending the Ben is reduced by one fourth since the path was made, but an active person can make the ascent and descent in an hour and a half less time by following the old track.

(*The Oban Times*, September 22, 1883)

BEN NEVIS MONDAY NIGHT: the first wheeled vehicle which ever ascended Ben Nevis did so today. Mr. Hugh MacDonald, coach proprietor, ascended with a spring cart especially made to suit the width of the path. It is to be used to carry provisions to the top. On this occasion it carried four hundredweight of coal. A large number of local people also ascended, and Mrs. Whyte of the Imperial Hotel, drove part of the way down from the summit. It is expected that the roof of the summit observatory will be completed on the tenth inst. On Friday and Saturday last there were six inches of snow on the summit and eight workmen slept in the Observatory and found it much more comfortable than the hut or the tents at the lake. Curiously enough a stag was seen bounding past the Observatory on Friday afternoon.

(*The Oban Times*, October 13, 1883)

Deep in winter on a spur of Ben Nevis

And stags weren't the only form of wildlife seen on the Ben.

Such an abundance of insect life on a mountain summit of such altitude is, in truth, very extraordinary; and the suggestion that they were swept up the gullies by warm currents of air from below is worthy of all acceptation as the only possible explanation of a phenomenon which on first announcement seems so strange as to be almost incredible. One thing is clear: the insects described as met with on the top of Ben Nevis are not those at home. They are foreign to such a habitat; are there by accident, and, so to speak, in spite of themselves. All the species identified by Mr. Thornley are inhabitants of the plains - not of Alpine heights. They are as much out of place on the top of Ben Nevis as if they were picked up on an ice-berg in sub-Arctic seas.

Of the various species of Coleoptera identified by Mr. Thornley not one is to be described as indigenous to a habitat of such altitude. One would like to know if the many hundreds of thousands of Aphides referred to by Mr. Bruce were all winged insects. If so, they were all males; and being winged, their presence on the topics is to be accounted for on the theory of upward currents of warm air through gully and gorge which wafted them to the top. If, however, any of the Aphides were wingless, then these were females; and as regards them the theory of upward rushes of warm air will not hold. A wingless Aphis could not be so exalted, and the presence of a single wingless Aphis on the top must be held to prove that Aphides at least are indigenous to their high level habitat. In May and June the female Aphis is wingless, and being wingless, could not possibly be wafted to the top by a current of air. If, on the contrary, all the Aphides were winged, then they were at that season all males, and the upward rushes of warm air from the base of the mountain will satisfactorily enough account for their presence on the summit.

In the collection transmitted to Mr. Thornley he found a few specimens of a not uncommon longicorn beetle - Rhagium Inquisitor. To account for the presence on the top of Ben Nevis of these longicorns, Mr. Thornley suggests that they may have been carried up in their caterpillar form in the logs of wood, undergoing their last stage of metamorphosis after the ascent, and of course there remaining. This is a very probable explanation of the presence on the top of the Ben of several of the species described, as well as of the Rhagium Inquisitor.

(*Inverness Courier*, October 15, 1897)

The New Instrument Room, Ben Nevis Observatory, 9.15p.m., Wiring the Daily Report, 3rd May, 1885.

And as the fascination with insects and animals continued, so, towards the end of the century, did the "mania" relating to the Ben. It manifested itself in many wonderful forms.

The *Fort William News*, a paper which was published for nearly two years at the end of the 1890s, regaled its readers as follows:

> The proprietors of Long John's Ben Nevis Distillery have published an amusing storyette of "two maids, four men and a Mountain: of Sunshine and Snow: of the Princess Shiela: of a Poet who never published: and of the Spell that the Spirit of the Mountain casts upon the Children of the Valleys."
>
> The party of six thus enumerated endeavour to break the record on Ben Nevis, but the "elements" are not favourable, and the record remains unbroken. The poet already alluded to had been communing with the Spirit of the Mountain, and on the evening preceding the ascent he read to the company in the hotel the following poem, written on the back of a laundry bill:-

If you are anxious for to shine in the mountaineering line,
as a record breaker bold.

You must cultivate a passion for a strong gymnastic
fashion in the Spartan way of old.

With the dumb-bells you must toy, and a boxing bout enjoy,
and swing an Indian club.

And profess a joy ecstatic for all pleasures aerobatic
and an early morning tub.

When your mountain you've selected, let it never be
suspected that your feat, perhaps, may fail:

Let your soul be full of daring, send your sole to
the repairing, and you'll be as right's the mail!

With a stout staff to assist you, there's no record will resist you,
when you've begun your task,

If you chance to be so happy as have "a wee bit drappie"
o' Long John in your flask.

And everyone will cry, when you've made the record fly -

If this Long John can inspire a man with such agilitee,

Why, what a very singularly good Long John this good Long John must be!

Ben Nevis *The Scottish Collection*   *Ronnie Weir*

Chapter 2

A Proud Centenary of Tradition

With thanks to

The Oban Times
& West Highland Times

The Ben Nevis Race and the West Highland Railway line through 1994-95 have been celebrating their centenaries, jointly and concurrently. The two events, the advent of the railway and the establishment of a unique sporting challenge now recognised the world over as the supreme test of athletic fitness, have given Fort William remarkable elements of an already fascinating background.

There is little doubt but that the opening of the West Highland Line on the Glorious Twelfth, August 12, 1894, contributed hugely to the development of the Race, never mind its contribution to Fort William and the West.

The 100 miles of the West Highland Railway between Craigendoran and Fort William were the longest length of line in Great Britain to be brought into service on the same date. 11 coaches hauled by 'West Highland Bogie' (North British Railways Class N, later London & North Eastern Railway Class D35) No 701 took the official party led by the Marchioness of Tweedale from Glasgow Queen Street to Fort William in some four hours and twenty minutes. The journey was the start of something very big indeed.

The opening was the culmination of one of the greatest feats of engineering of its day. Some 5,000 men had been employed in the building of the railway. The first sod had been cut by Lord Abinger near the Ben Nevis Distillery on October 23, 1889.

(Top) Lord Abinger cutting the first sod.

(Centre) The Ceremonial arrival of the first train at Fort William.

(Bottom) Fort William station, interior.

The difficulty of constructing a railway up the glens and across the boggy wastes of Rannoch Moor in the often severe Highland climate is not hard to imagine. Viaducts, tunnels and a solitary snow shed were all constructed as the brave souls building the line battled with the elements. Much of the work was done by hand tools - supplemented by steam machinery, which at the time was quite novel.

The demanding topography required an astonishing 617 bridges, along with 12 tunnels, to climb over mountain and moor. This epic construction was a costly enterprise, requiring capital of some £10,000 per mile, a sizeable sum in Victorian times.

It is no wonder then that *The Oban Times* joined in the celebrations in some style on Saturday, August 18, 1894:

A glimpse of Fort William

The new West Highland Line just opened for general traffic is characterised by engineering experts to be one of the 'biggest' railway undertakings inaugurated in this country during the last quarter of a century.

From a utilitarian point of view, it is an undertaking fraught with possibilities of the highest importance to a large section of country hitherto cut off, or imperfectly served, with speedy means of communication with the markets of the South.

To the lover of scenic beauty, again, and to the most impressionable among the tourist race, it will afford an infinite amount of pleasure, inasmuch as it traverses - as has been aptly described - an area which reveals an ever-changing panorama of vast lakes and mighty mountains, weird wastes, and beautiful glens, and a tract of country laden with historic associations and memories of the past.

If it was a 'Far Cry to Lochawe' till the shrill whistle of the locomotive awoke the echoes of that picturesque lake, it was still a more distant 'cry' to the historic and legend haunted region of Lochiel.

Now, however, by means of the iron horse, the worthy citizens of Glasgow and Edinburgh may partake of a late breakfast at home, and still be able to enjoy in comfort an early dinner in 'Far Lochaber', under the frowning shadow of Ben Nevis - the monarch amongst British mountains.

THE FIRST SOD of the new line was cut in the latter part of 1889 by the late Lord Abinger, and the construction of the hundred and one miles has therefore taken close upon five years to complete.

North British Railway Company.

OFFICE OF SUPERINTENDENT OF THE LINE,
EDINBURGH, *9th August,* 1894.

PRIVATE.
No.— E 29—90.

OPENING OF THE WEST HIGHLAND RAILWAY

BY THE MOST HONOURABLE

THE MARCHIONESS OF TWEEDDALE,

On SATURDAY, 11th AUGUST 1894.

A Special Train, consisting of 11 Vehicles, conveying Guests on the occasion of the Official Opening of the West Highland Railway, will be run from Glasgow (Queen Street High Level Station) to Fort-William and back, as under :—

			1 a.m.					2 p.m.	3
Glasgow (Queen Street High Level)	...	depart	8 15	Fort-William (Temporary Platform)	depart		3 55		
Craigendoran	...	„	8 53	Spean Bridge	...	„	4 14		
Garelochhead	...	„	9 12	Inverlair	...	„	4 36		
Arrochar and Tarbet	...	„	9 36						
				Rannoch { arrive			5 18		
Crianlarich	...	„	10 15	{ depart			5 25		
Rannoch	...	pass	11 15	Crianlarich	...	„	6 22		
Inverlair	...	depart	11 58	Ardlui	...	„	6 42		
			p.m.	Arrochar and Tarbet		„	7 0		
Spean Bridge	...	„	12 16	Garelochhead	...	„	7 25		
Banavie Junction	...	„	12 32	Craigendoran	...	„	7 42		
Fort-William (Temporary Platform)	...	arrive	12 35			{ arrive	8 8		
				Cowlairs No. Jun. { depart			8 10	8 12	
				Do. East	„	„	...	8 14	
				Cowlairs Station		„	8 12	...	
				Glasgow (Queen Street High Level)	arrive		8 20	...	
				Polmont	...	pass	...	8 42	
				Haymarket	...	depart	...	9 10	
				Edinburgh (Suburban Platform) { arrive			...	9 18	
				{ depart			...	9 22	
				Longniddry	...	„	...	9 44	
				Haddington	...	arrive	...	9 56	

No. 1.—Meets at Arrochar the 6-20 a.m. Passenger Train from Fort-William to Glasgow, and at Inverlair the 11-15 a.m. Passenger Train from Fort-William to Glasgow. Leading Engine to be uncoupled at Banavie Junction, and the Train brought to a stand on the outside of the Ornamental Arch to be erected 15 feet short of Fort-William Home Signal.

No. 2.—Meets at Inverlair the 12-42 p.m. Passenger Train from Glasgow to Fort-William, and at Ardlui the 4-50 p.m. Passenger Train from Glasgow to Fort-William. The Guard of the Train must be prepared to attach Tail Lamp to the last Vehicle of the Glasgow portion of the Train from Cowlairs North Junction.

No. 3.—Three Vehicles for Edinburgh and Haddington on the rear of No. 2 Special will be detached at Cowlairs North, and an Engine, Guard, and Van must be in readiness to take them forward. Station-master, Edinburgh, to provide the Guard.

This Train is intended to precede from Cowlairs East Junction the 8-0 p.m. Express from Glasgow (Queen Street High Level), and it is important that it be worked punctually.

Station-masters will deliver a copy of this Advice to each of the Block Signalmen, Signal Porters, Gate-Keepers, and all other necessary parties whose names appear in their respective Pay Bills.

D. DEUCHARS, Superintendent of the Line.

When originally mooted, it was estimated that the line would cost somewhere about £600,000, but from many unforeseen causes which from time to time arose that sum has been considerably exceeded.

The engineers were Messrs. Formans and MacColl, Glasgow; and the contractors for the whole line the famous Messrs Lucas and Aird, the chief and representative of which was Mr. H. B. Tarry, a gentleman whose energy, tact and ability were displayed in high degree, and whose duties during the progress of the work were arduous and incessant.

The principal sub-contractors were Messrs Findlay of Motherwell, who have constructed about four hundred bridges of steel along the course of the line; and Messrs G B Smith and Company, Glasgow, who have erected the fencing; the signals being supplied by Messrs Saxby and Farmer, London. There are altogether nineteen.

STATIONS ON THE LINE namely Craigendoran, Upper Helensburgh, Rhu, Shandon, Glen Douglas, Garelochead, Arrochar and Tarbet, Ardlui, Crianlaraich, Tyndrum, Bridge of Orchy, Gorten, Rannoch, Corrour, Inverlair, Roy Bridge, Spean Bridge, Fort William and Banavie.

The majority of stations have been built on the island principle, and the ranges of booking offices and waiting-rooms on each are picturesque erections of Swiss design.

For the traffic on the line, special engines and carriages have been constructed at the North British Railway Company's works at Cowlairs, Glasgow.

Altogether, nine locomotives have been built in a manner adapted for the hilly nature of the route, and each (with tender and load) weighs 75 tons.

Four complete trains have also been constructed, each train consisting of a first-class carriage, two third-class carriages, and a brake van. Both the first and third-class carriages are a combination of the compartment, saloon, and corridor carriage.

Two windows have been specially arranged for affording the best possible and most uninterrupted views of the scenery. On each window blind there is a map of the route, and the interior panels of the carriages are ornamented with photographic views of the points of beauty and grandeur along the line.

THE STARTING POINT of the new line is at Craigendoran - an offshoot of Helensburgh, and the steamboat station of the North British Railway, with which latter system it is linked with Glasgow, Edinburgh, and London. From Craigendoran a short run of two miles brings the traveller to the station at Upper Helensburgh, where the first stoppage is made.

Curving northwards, a beautiful glimpse of the Clyde and Gareloch is opened up.

The placid Firth of Clyde stretches to the southward, with Rosneath Castle, hemmed partly in by a clump of famous firs, and backed by the rugged mountains of Argyll, lying on the western side, while the Gareloch waters extend to the north.

Sweeping along the elevated shoreland a series of stations fringe the water's edge. Rhu, a pleasant resort dotted with tree-embowered mansions and villas owned by Glasgow merchants, comes first, and is quickly succeeded by Shandon, a famous rendezvous in Summer time, and altogether a delightful sylvan retreat.

As the line proceeds along the Gareloch the scenery all round combines many of the finest features of Highland and Lowland sea and landscape.

On both sides the loch is shut in by low hills, right and left, covered with foliage; and so deep and still are its waters , and so free are the hills from magnetic influences, that it is the favourite place for the testing of ship's compasses, and a popular place for vessels lying up. Indeed it is said that three millions worth of shipping at present lie there resting. At Garelochhead there is another station for the sheltered little village of that name.

Leaving the Gareloch behind, the line goes over the River Fruin; and as it runs down towards the junction of Loch Goil and Loch Long, and continues its course on the eastern side of the latter waterway, the scenery assumes an aspect of increasing grandeur, the eye first resting on the beautiful arm of the Firth, then on the bold hills and wild hill glens along its sides, and, finally, on the serried edge of mountains known as the 'Duke's Bowing Green'.

Travelling on northward, the sparsely-clad vale of Mallin and the richly wooded Glen Douglas are in turn passed on the east side, and on the opposite side a glimpse is caught of Glencroe, which leads to Loch Fyne and Inveraray; and between them, ranging round the head of Loch Long, a perfect sea of mountain peaks is to be seen,

Arrochar, head of Loch Long (from railway)

Glen Falloch

with the celebrated 'Cobbler' conspicuous among them.

With the view of accommodating the traffic of the two districts of Arrochar at the head of Loch Long, and Tarbet, on the north-west shore of Loch Lomond, a station has been placed midway between them, and a more attractive centre for tourist traffic is well nigh impossible to conceive. It is a paradise of mountain, wood and watery scenery.

On the Arrochar side there is the charmingly-situated hamlet of that name, half girt by trees and overshadowed by mountain peaks; and on the other there is the queen of Scottish lakes, dominated by Ben Lomond.

To add still further to the fascination of the district, the traveller is also in the very heart of a country redolent with clan feuds, and within view of the territories over which the Colquhouns, the MacFarlanes, and the MacGregors held sway.

All around Arrochar and Tarbet, and a long way north along the loch, was the country of Clan MacFarlane, a wild race of freebooters as they were called, whose habit of descending on the Lowlands by night gave the local name of "MacFarlane's lantern" to the moon.

On the eastern side of the loch lies the MacGregor country - the home of the Gregarach or Clan Alpine, from which they were so ruthlessly driven out, when their very name was prescribed and their possessions confiscated on account of their turbulence.

From Tarbet, Loch Lomond winds northwards like a river amid lofty hills, and apart from the magnificent views which are obtained down the loch as the railway proceeds the Falls of Inversnaid are to be seen.

From Ardlui, which is twenty-seven miles from Craigendoran, the railway takes its way through the lovely Glen Falloch.

In the plantations which clothe the lower declivities of the glen the remnants of some old Scottish firs - said to be part of the original Caledonian Forest, which stretched as far as Oban - still stands as an interesting feature, more particularly to arboriculturists.

Railway Viaduct at Crianlarich

During its course through Glen Falloch, the line is continuously overlooked by high hills, with Ben More standing out in the distance, and on emerging from the Glen a run over a stretch of moorland completes the journey to Crianlarich, where, on a lofty viaduct, the line crosses the Callander and Oban Railway, and proceeds to Tyndrum.

At Crianlarich - forty-one miles from Craigendoran - a junction is made with the line to Oban, and passengers at this point can proceed direct to the far-famed 'Charing Cross' of the Highlands.

Leaving Crianlarich an embankment, thirty feet high and stretching right across Strathfillan, carries the line to the north side of the valley. It was here in the early days that St. Fillan, one of the first preachers of the Gospel in the north, came down the Glen, journeying from Iona, and established in the Strath a Culdee Church, now know as St. Fillan's Chapel.

Here also was the scene of the battle of Dalrigh, inseparably connected with the name of Robert the Bruce and the MacDougalls of Lorn. Here the line turns westward, running along the side of the hill parallel to the Callander and Oban Railway to Tyndrum, where there is a station.

In this portion the line continues to rise, and passes over Inverhaggernie and Auchtertyre viaducts. The bridge over the Auchtertyre Burn, three miles above Crianlarich, is the most important work on this section.

It is about 120 feet above the water, with a central span of 101 feet, and two on each side of 66 feet each.

Proceeding north-west from Tyndrum for about a mile, the railway continues to rise till it reaches the march between Perthshire and Argyllshire at a summit of 1024 feet above the sea level.

Looking down Strathfillan

The route is now, with a slight variation, due north along the base of a series of high mountains till Orchy Bridge is reached, and in this distance of six or seven miles there is a gradual fall of nearly 200 feet.

After passing the summit, the most prominent object in the landscape is the great hog-backed Ben Doran towering in front, with Ben Vurie and Ben Castle to the right; and this group, with the intervening valleys between them, make together a grand spectacle.

It is at this particular point that the slight variation from the straight line occurs. Ben Castle, which is in the middle of three mountains, recedes somewhat from the line of the other two; and round the semi-circle thus formed the railway sweeps, clinging to the bases of the Bens with the seemingly almost perpendicular sides impending over it, and the valleys between it by means of bridges, from which rare views are commanded up the glens.

This round occupies something like a couple of miles and then the railway goes straight northwards and downwards, Bridge of Orchy being nearly 200 feet lower that the summit of the march between Perthshire and Argyllshire.

From the last mentioned station, Bridge of Orchy, the famous Orchy is seen stretching for miles away to the south-west, enclosed in rugged wild mountains.

From Orchy Bridge station, the main road to Glencoe may be taken, and this is also the stopping place for Loch Tula, noted for its angling attractions. In the vicinity the Gaelic poet, Duncan Ban MacIntyre, was born.

The loch is overlooked by the railway, and at its head there are the ruins of the Black Castle at Achallader, a lonely keep round which in bygone centuries many a bloody clan fight was waged.

Adhering to the course of the River Tulla for a short distance, the line goes on through Crannoch Wood, another relic of the old Caledonian Forest, and over a piece of moorland to Gorten.

Between these stations the Black Mount deer forest of the Marquis of Breadlabane extends, covering some 80,000 acres, and ranking as one of the finest sporting grounds in the kingdom.

The line is now in the very heart of the most impressive Highland scenery; and, after a run of a few miles from Gorten, the heathery waste known as Rannoch Moor is entered upon.

This moor is well described as the largest and dreariest tract of its kind in Scotland - "an open, monotonous, silent, black extent of desert; a vast region of bog and morass, with a few dreary pools and one long dreary lake, some ditchy naked lines of dark water courses, whose coarse dark features are in rueful sympathy with humours of the sable sea of moss."

The moor is some twenty miles long, and is a thousand feet above sea level. It is also, as may naturally be assumed, a valuable sporting ground.

In addition to its sporting attractions, it has also a literary interest. Robert Louis Stevenson, in his famous novel 'Kidnapped,' has described in masterly language the flight of Alan Breck and young David Balfour across the Rannoch Moor after the Appin murder.

To cross the fourteen miles of Rannoch Moor was the most difficult part of the undertaking, as the moor is so inaccessible that it had to be telescoped from end to end.

Through this 'howling wilderness' as it had been termed, the railway runs almost due north, passing over the Gauer (which connects Loch Lydock with Loch Rannoch) by means of a high viaduct, and then curves round to the north-west, where it attains the summit of 1350 feet above the level of the sea at the bottom of Ben Bhreic, and shortly we come in view of Loch Treig, famous as an angling resort.

Near the northern end of the loch is situated a small island, otherwise described as 'The Council Island', where, it is said, the chiefs of the Clan Cameron and the Clan MacKintosh used to meet in conference when any dispute arose between the two clans, and it was a question of peace or war.

This solitary and detached spot was chosen as a place of meeting in order that the chiefs might be safe from treacherous ambushes.

At the head of the loch there is the station of Inverlair, and then the line changes its course and runs along the Spean Valley by way of Glens Roy and Spean, where lovely views of Ben Nevis and Lochaber district are opened up.

Loch Treig (looking towards Inverlair)

Glen Roy, apart from its gloomy wildness, is noted for its geologic phenomena, 'the parallel roads', or terraces cut by the shore waters of a lake that once filled Glen Roy.

Near Roy Bridge there is situated Keppoch House, the scene of the Keppoch murder, and the terrible vengeance which was meted out to the murderers.

Near the bridge there is also Mullroy Hill, on which the last clan battle was fought in Scotland; and, not far off from this place, Viscount Dundee held a council of Jacobite chiefs in 1689 before marching on to Killiecrankie, where he met his death.

The line proceeds on through the Spean valley, and passes the ruined castle of Inverlochy, of which many a tale might be told, and the distillery where the far-famous 'Long John' whisky is manufactured.

From this point the line comes under the shadow of the Great Ben looming up to over four thousand feet above sea level, and thence through the site of the old fort, erected to overawe the clans, and which gave the name to the present town of Fort William.

Immediately the terminal station is reached after a delightful four and a-half hours' run from Glasgow through a magnificently picturesque section of country embraced in four separate counties, namely, Dumbarton, Perth, Argyll and Inverness.

'The little township of Fort William,' says the writer of that admirably got-up work, 'Mountain, Moor and Loch,' 'has sprung up around the fort, which was originally built by General Monk, in Cromwell's time, as a rude fortification of turf, to act as a base for the troops sent to keep in subjection Evan Dhu of Locheil,

The view from the pier, showing Station Square in the mid-fifties.

the Chief of the Camerons, who stood out like a Scottish Hereward against the forces of the Commonwealth, long after the other clans had submitted.

Many a fierce skirmish between Locheil and the Sassenach red-coats took place around Fort William and Inverlochy, the Highlanders generally getting the best of it, as is recorded in Scott's 'Tales of a Grandfather'.

Spean Bridge

In the time of William the Third the fort was rebuilt in its present form (or rather its late form, for the railway works have cut much of it up) by General MacKay, who was afterwards defeated by Viscount Dundee at Killiecrankie.

It was a strong fortification of its kind, with ditches, glacis, and ravelin, of which portions may yet be seen, mounting fifteen twelve pounders, and with a regular garrison of about a hundred men: while, in times of trouble, many more soldiers were thrown into it. Both in the '15 and the '45 it was besieged by Jacobites, but never was taken.

Afterwards, when the present fort was built, the people were encouraged to erect houses there, to form a village to be a sutlery to it. They might build where and how they liked, only the houses were to be composed of turf and wattle, so as to be easily set on fire in case of a rising, or of an enemy effecting a lodgement there.

This village was demolished, and then the people began to build at the seaside, where the lower streets of the town are now, and the free charters given then account for the irregularity of the buildings, which, from the sea, look so disorderly.

Various attempts have been made to rename the town after it was raised to the dignity of a burgh of barony. First it was called Maryburgh, in honour of William's consort; but it remained Fort William, in honour of William himself.

Later, the Duke of Gordon was made a superior of the township, and it was called Gordonsburgh; but it remained Fort William.

Afterwards, Sir Duncan Cameron became superior, and called it Duncansburgh; but it remained Fort William.

Within the past few weeks Parliamentary sanction has been given to the extension of the line from fort William to Mallaig on the Inverness-shire coast; and this section, when completed, will accommodate the trio of interests - fishing, agricultural and tourist - which the line was intended to serve when first projected.

Considerable importance, indeed, may be attached to the extension just sanctioned. It will not only increase the revenue of the line now finished, but afford easy means of transit to the large cities of the south.

The extension line will proceed by way of Banavie, the entrance to the Caledonian Canal, where a steamer is caught direct for Inverness.

A super Sprinter weaves its way towards Ben Nevis and Fort William at Banavie, following the line taken by some early runners in the Ben Race at the turn of last century.

The beautiful views which illustrate this sheet are taken from that splendidly got-up work just published, entitled, 'Mountain, Moor, and Loch.' For the use of the blocks we are indebted to the publishers, Sir Joseph Causon and Sons, London, who, in the most courteous manner, have placed them at our disposal.

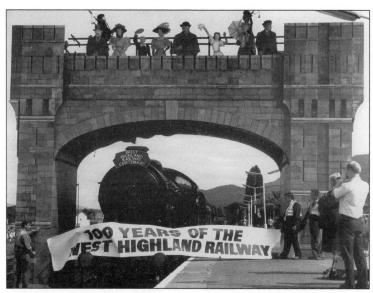

Centenary event train going through archway, August, 1994.
Dave Allaway, The Oban Times.

For further reading on the history of the West Highland Line, see "*The West Highland Railway*" by John Thomas, first published in 1965, but now much up-dated; also "*100 Years of the West Highland Railway*", by John MacGregor, in association with ScotRail (published by ScotRail, 1994).

To mark the joint centenary celbrations of ScotRail and the Ben Nevis Race, the 1994 event was appropriately sponsored by ScotRail. Paul Sommerville, Commercial Director, was the official starter.

A late nineteenth century view of Ben Nevis.

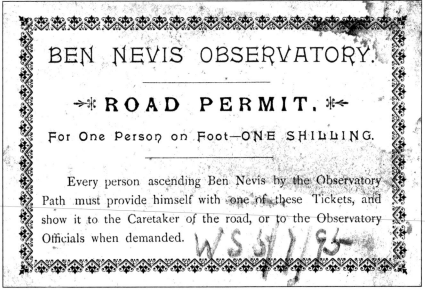

This permit, marked WS 5/9/95, is believed to have been Willie Swan's. Courtesy of Jimmy Murdoch, Alma Road, Fort William.

Chapter 3

1895-1909
For sport, not for reward

"A foot-race from the post office at Fort-William to the top of Ben Nevis and back, was an event which helped considerably to vary the routine of things at the Observatory. Strength of muscle and physical endurance are qualities which seldom fail to call forth admiration; but when these are employed in foolhardy and dangerous exploits, their possessor is surely acting in opposition to the laws of nature."

Such was William Kilgour's reaction to what he later described as the "mania" which suddenly captured the imagination of the good folk of Lochaber and, indeed, many from much further afield. Not content with getting to the top of Britain's highest mountain, the object quickly became to get there quicker than anyone else. All of a sudden records became the vogue - the oldest person to the top, the youngest, the first woman and, inevitably, the fastest ..... and so it went on.

Kilgour was not impressed:

> "There doubtless is a qualified degree of honour in being able to sprint up and down such a mountain as Ben Nevis in two hours and a half, but is the game really worth the candle? What object is to be gained thereby? Verily, athletics are extending if such a departure is destined to come within the category."

Goodness only knows what the redoubtable Kilgour would make of events now with 500 runners making the annual ascent of the Ben in 1985. But when 27-year old William Swan, a local hairdresser, dog breeder, sporting buff and general man about town, made his legendary first timed ascent of the mountain at the end of September, 1895, he achieved much more than celebrity status. Cycling to the front of the Ben, he established a record which is to this day, for a variety of reasons, still unbeaten.

(There is some debate about the precise date of this first timed run, but the evidence of contemporary sources such as *The Oban Times* and *Inverness Courier* suggests fairly precisely, that Friday 27 September or Monday September 30 was the occasion. Funnily enough, the Wednesday of the first of these weeks was the autumn holiday in Fort William, but wasn't chosen for the ascent).

(On Monday) Mr William Swan, tobacconist here, ascended Ben Nevis with the object of establishing a record. The day was exceedingly hot and unsuitable for mountaineering, but, notwithstanding, Mr Swan managed to reach the summit, and, after drinking a cup of Bovril, returned to Fort William in the incredibly short space of 2 hours 41 minutes. This is believed to be a record.

(*Inverness Courier*, Friday, October 4, 1895)

41

Meanwhile, *The Oban Times* of October 5 reports that "two Ladies, the Misses Napier", made the ascent of Tower Ridge on the Friday evening of the week before. The event was recorded as "the first occasion on which lady mountaineers have ascended the mountain by the precipice route."

As to the origins of the "mania" (as Kilgour referred to it) of running the timed ascent, these must remain a mystery, but at the end of the day the simplest explanation seems to be man's quest for a challenge and his will to achieve, and better, what no other has done.

Horses were used to transport materials to the top of the Ben as the path was built to the top.

But what of Lochaber, and in particular the town of Fort William in which this mania took hold? In 1871, according to the Census, there were just over 1,200 souls in Fort William; ten years later, the number had swelled to 1856, 65% of whom were Gaelic speakers. Indeed 48 could speak only Gaelic.

The Census of 1871 reported that in one district: *"the High Street of Fort William with the lanes, closes and squares to the south side of the said High Street, and the houses to the east of the said village to the burn at the Carding Mill, including the Fort and the Parade"* - there were 117 houses and 843 people; in the other district, *"Low Street and Middle Street lanes and closes leading from the north side of High Street to the sea shore from the Spout Burn to east of the Gas Works on the west"* - there were 51 houses and a population of 360. The population of **1,203** persons lived in **168** houses - an average of 7.1 to a house.

The last remaining part of the Old Fort, Fort William. The houses, which were demolished in 1948, were originally occupied by the officers. In a ground-floor room of the nearest house the preparations were made for the massacre of Glencoe. The shore wall in front of the houses is now all that is left of the Old Fort.

Gateway at the entrance to the Craigs burial-ground, Fort William. Originally, it formed the entrance to the Fort. Behind the left-hand seat appears the rock from which Prince Charlie's forces bombarded the Fort in 1746.

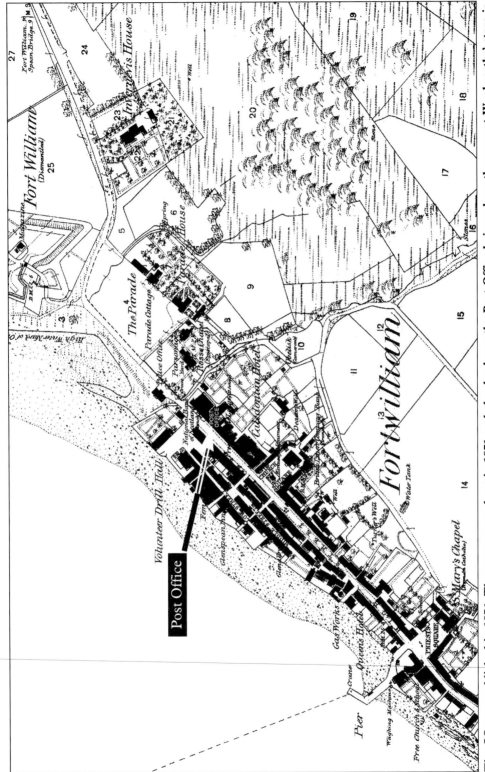

The OS map published in 1876. The survey was done in 1871 and clearly shows the Post Office being where the current Woolworths' store is, beside the Royal Bank of Scotland - ironically perhaps, almost directly across the road from the site of the modern Post Office. This Post Office was overtaken eventually by the site at 88 High Street.

Early postcard, c.1900

It is worth pointing out, for all the interest in running up to the top of the Ben, other, more adventurous methods, had already been tried.

> **BEN NEVIS MONDAY NIGHT: the first wheeled vehicle which ever ascended Ben Nevis did so today. Mr. Hugh MacDonald, coach proprietor, ascended with a spring cart especially made to suit the width of the path. It is to be used to carry provisions to the top. On this occasion it carried four hundredweight of coal. A large number of local people also ascended, and Mrs. Whyte of the Imperial Hotel, drove part of the way down from the summit. It is expected that the roof of the summit observatory will be completed on the tenth inst. On Friday and Saturday last there were six inches of snow on the summit and eight workmen slept in the Observatory and found it much more comfortable than the hut or the tents at the lake. Curiously enough a stag was seen bounding past the Observatory on Friday afternoon.**
>
> *(**The Oban Times,** October 13, 1883)*

The first motor car to the top of the Ben was to be a model T Ford driven by Henry Alexander in 1911. George Simpson drove an Austin 7 up in 1928 in a record time of 7 hours 23 minutes. He made his descent in just under two hours and then drove the car back to Edinburgh! Others made the ascent by motor-bike, and Donald MacDougall, Fort William's town crier or "bellman" for 56 years, showed off his strength by pushing a 73lb wheelbarrow up in 1887.

Donald MacDougall, "the Bellman"

Henry Alexander on his descent, 1911.

There was no shortage of pastimes in Lochaber at the time. In his novel *"In Far Lochaber"* written in the 1870s, William Black portrays the town thus:

"Peace reigns in Fort William now. Lochiel has no trouble with his clansmen, the Government has no trouble with Lochiel; the garrison buildings have been turned into private dwellings; women sit on the grassy bastion of the fort and knit stockings, sheltering themselves from the sun with an old umbrella; in the square are wooden benches for looking on at tossing the caber, putting the stone and other Highland games; in the fosse is an excellent crop of potatoes and cabbages; and just outside there is a trimly kept bowling green in which the club members practice the gentle art of reaching the tee when the waning afternoon releases them from their desk or counter."

Shinty appears to have been the main sport of the day, with the annual New Year games particularly, attracting the attention of a considerable crowd. In January 1880 - on the 12th to be precise - a "very keen" game was played at Fort William between the Blarmachfoldach tenants and Achintore and Druimarbin tenants. The "very stalwart" appearance of both teams was noted in *The Highlander,* and it was reported that "the best of feeling prevailed and many were wearing Highland dress", fortified, no doubt by some of the *Dew of Ben Nevis,* given that it was a New Year match in the traditional custom!

Alex Gillespie

And the Ben was to the fore in the ancient and noble game by virtue of the fact that there was a club bearing its name. The Ben Nevis uniform was navy blue knickerbockers, black and white jerseys and stockings.

The Town and County Directory for the North of Scotland (Inverness, 1885) lists the office-bearers of the Ben Nevis Club as President: D. MacPherson, Glen Nevis; Captain, Alex MacDonald; Vice-Captain, John Young; Secretary, Wm Davidson; Treasurer, A. Young.

The same booklet (an invaluable snap-shot of Fort William and other Highland areas at the time) describes Fort William, with a population of 1,562, as "a centre for tourists". Amongst the other bodies listed are the Belford Hospital Trust, Lochaber Curling Club, Bowling Club, Debating Society and Mutual Improvement Society, the Masonic Lodge and the United Templar Society.

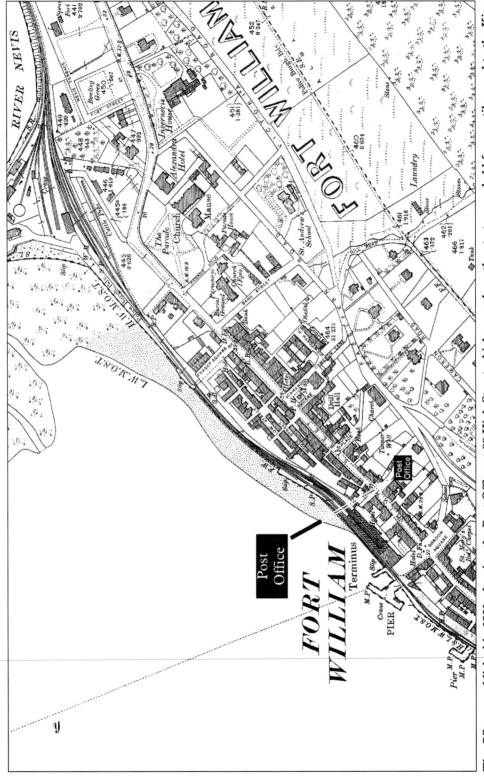

The OS map published in 1901, showing the Post Office at 88 High Street which was where the starts were held from until moved to the King George V Park. The Post Office was where the mile stone was, making the distance calculated for the race very precise. The survey for this map was done in 1899, the previous one shown earlier in 1871. William Swan would have started from here.

FORT WILLIAM - SHINTY MATCH

On Monday (which was observed as New Year's day) a shinty match was played on a field at Annat by a team of 15 of the Ben-Nevis (Fort William) Shinty Club and an equal number of the Ardgour men. This match may be said to be the match of the season as it is a match between counties - Inverness and Argyll. The ball was thrown up in midfield about 1p.m. About 20 minutes thereafter the Ben-Nevis Club secured the first goal by a well-directed blow. The Ardgour men now worked with great determination, and in about 10 minutes placed a goal to their credit. It was now the turn of the Ben-Nevis Club, and in 15 minutes they scored a second goal, and after a hard struggle they placed a third goal to their credit. The Ardgour men now struggled hard to equalise matters, but the Ben-Nevis players proved too strong for them, and ultimately succeeded in placing a fourth goal to their credit. On time being called, the match stood thus - Ben-Nevis Club, four goals; Ardgour Team, one goal. Rain fell heavily throughout the match. The Ben-Nevis team were dressed in their uniforms - navy blue knickerbockers, black and white jerseys, black and white stockings, and a neat cap - and looked smart, indeed. Mr. Donald P. MacDonald, Invernevis, acted as umpire for the Ben-Nevis Club, while Mr. Allan Rankin officiated in the same capacity for the Ardgour team. The match throughout went on quietly and harmoniously. At the close of the match both teams were treated to refreshments on the field. Notwithstanding the unfavourable weather the crowd of spectators was immense, and heartily cheered the players of both sides when praise was merited.

(*Inverness Courier,* February 5, 1882)

Eddie Campbell, Ben Race runner extra-ordinaire, officiating at the Camanachd Association's centenary shinty match, Kingussie, April 3, 1993.

There were four bakers in the town at the time, three banks, two blacksmiths, a bookseller, seven "Boot and Shoemakers", five carpenters, three coal merchants, two china merchants, the famous distiller D. P. MacDonald, two druggists (one of which was Peter MacFarlane); five fleshers; no less than 22 grocers and eight hotels, one of which was the Ben Nevis - proprietor R. M. Shankland. All this as well as the Post Office, an assortment of painters, solicitors, tailors, watchmakers, vintners, saddlers and two surgeons. Interestingly perhaps, no mention is made of William Swan, tobacconist and hairdresser, who was to leave his mark indelibly on the town in ten years' time.

Willie Swan, outside his shop, opposite MacFarlane the Chemist's.

The Fort William of my youth was not a thing of beauty. The foreshore was a disgrace. But with the coming of the railway and the march of civilisation and improvement the place is changed out of recognition. "Maryburgh, drunken town" was how Hugh Barclay described it - and he had reason for giving it such a description. It had in my early days about a dozen licensed houses. This was a great decrease from still earlier times. My mother told me there were twenty three drinking places within her recollection while at Nevis Bridge and Lochy Bridge there were licences also."

"A Boyhood in An Gearasdan", in Transactions of the Gaelic Society of Inverness. Vol LVII, pp234 and 237.

Looking East c.1900. Runners leaving the Post Office at 88 High Street would run through here and back. The original Post Office was in the distance where the trees are on the right hand side.

Poaching was apparently another traditional custom and quite common in the Fort William area of the time. The late Principal John MacLeod's recollections of the area (he was born in Fort William on March 25, 1872) were recounted by his grandson Jeff at a meeting of the Gaelic Society of Inverness in March, 1992, in a talk entitled "A Boyhood in An Gearasdan ":

> **"The catching of salmon in the loch was not looked upon by the fisher folk as poaching. The landed folks looked upon it in another light. Popular feeling sided with the fishermen. There used to be some fine poachers who knew how to hunt the stag. They might be taken up for trespassing in pursuit of the game. They had aristocratic if nocturnal tastes in the matter of selecting their quarry. It used to be said that Sandy MacEwan from Inverness and Jock the Piper, a Skyeman, the son of Mary MacPherson the Skye poetess, knew a good deal about these things. They were both said to be men of skill. Tales went about in regard to the prowess of the old priest Coll MacDonald as an undiscovered salmon fisherman in his early days in Brae Lochaber and his unmortified fondness for a cut of venison of his own killing when he was a priest in Fort William. He used to drive down to Ballachulish to hold a service there on Sabbath afternoon. He saw time and again a stag within easy reach of his gun not far from the gamekeeper's place near a clump of trees. The chance was too much for him. So one day he took his gun with him and as he was driving home from there, sure enough, was the stag within shot. There was a risk as the gamekeeper's house was so near. He came out of his trap, stalked and bagged his quarry. But the sound of the shot brought the keeper at full speed. The priest had not quite got into his trap but had hid his gun and was adjusting his clothes. He pointed beyond the wood and sent the keeper off in chase of the poacher. This gave him time to get the stag into his trap and get off before the keeper appeared on the scene again.**

(Transactions of the Gaelic Society of Inverness. **Vol LVII, 256-257).**

The *Inverness Courier* of March 21, 1893 reports that a certain Mr MacEwen of Inverlochy was fined the sum of 20 shillings with expenses of 25 shillings for a similar indiscretion. The report is accompanied by a note that teams representing Spean Bridge and Fort William played a shinty match in Glen Nevis the previous Saturday. Fort William had won by four hails to nil.

Curling was also popular at this time - Lochaber v Spean Bridge in a match at Glen Nevis c 1890. Curling was still taking place there in the 1950s.

And so it came to pass that for whatever reason, one William Swan completed what is now referred to as "the first authentic performance" of the Ben Nevis race. The next few years would see a fascinating series of runs undertaken by an intriguing set of individuals.

The route to the top then would have been much as it is now - the five miles or thereby of the bridle path, zig-zagging up the mountain, with a gradient of 1 in 5 at many points. The route down is that chosen by the individual - the quickest and not always the safest - some fourteen to fifteen miles in all, depending on where the starting point was taken.

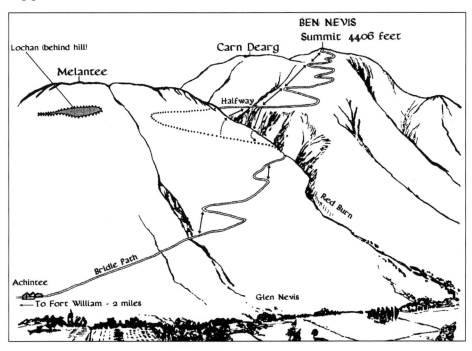

To make the ascent comfortably and with the least output of exertion, one should wear a pair of strong "tackety" boots, provide himself with a stout walking stick, and be clad as lightly as possible. A lemon and a few biscuits will not constitute a heavy knapsack, and these rations have frequently proved themselves of the utmost service in an emergency. Unless the pangs of hunger become excessive, it is well to refrain from eating during the climb, and imperatively more so to eschew water. Thirst is the constant companion of the quasi mountaineer, but the craving must be fought against all hazards, and it will usually be found that a little of the lemon juice will act as a panacea. A resolution should be formed prior to starting, never to rest on the journey up, as the oftener one sits down, the harder it becomes to proceed in the rarefied atmosphere. Of course with some - ladies especially - this is out of the question, and no rules for their guidance need be laid down. Though prescribed, such maxims would probably be disregarded in any case, so it is as well to steer clear of the possibility of being censured. The fair sex, the broken-winded and the rheumatic must therefore do their own sweet will on Ben Nevis. A large percentage of seemingly incapables reach the top, but in many cases the waste of energy in doing so is bound to have detrimental side effects.

(Kilgour, *Twenty Years*, pp11-12)

Apart from his interest in football, William Swan was also involved with the fledgling Fort William Shinty Club. Pictured here (second from the left, rear) after Fort William had won the Campbell Cup in 1912.

Mr Swan was also a dog breeder of some note and travelled widely to shows. A clean-cut English terrier of his - Nevendon Rogue - won a prize at Montrose. His fox-terrier "Snowball" was also a prize-winner at Southend on Sea and again at Woolwich.

The officials in the picture are (left to right): Alec MacDonald (Dalnuaran, Club Secretary), Mr Swan, Mr Marshall (of Marshall & Pearson), Sandy Campbell (Solicitor), Duncan Cameron (the old Fort). Players: (Left to right, back row) Ewan Kennedy, Mr Livingstone, Donald Kennedy. Front: Coll MacDonald (Achintee), James Foster, Mr R. Bull.

Detrimental side effects there may have been (as Kilgour would have it at any rate) as a result of the Race, but all of a sudden, largely due to the advent of the railway and the influx of visitors to the area, the top of Ben Nevis was the place to be.

Over 700 visitors climbed Ben Nevis during September. The refreshment rooms on the summit were closed on Monday last, that being the recognised end of the season. It appears that the number of visitors who climbed the mountain in June and July was much greater than on previous years, but in August and September there was a decrease in numbers who made the ascent as compared with the corresponding period last year, for which, no doubt, the inclement weather was accountable. Two ladies, the Misses Napier accompanied by Messrs Napier and Bell of the Scottish Mountaineering Club, made the ascent of the Tower Ridge, Ben Nevis last Friday evening. This is the first occasion on which lady mountaineers have ascended the mountain by the precipice route.

(*The Oban Times*, Saturday, October 5, 1895)

William Swan's first timed ascent and descent was made in two hours and forty-one minutes. He is understood to have started from the Post Office at 10am, cycled to the foot of the mountain and was back at the Post Office at 12.55pm after remaining at the top (where he apparently fortified himself with a cup of Bovril) for 14 minutes.

William Swan in later life, outside his High Street Premises.

The point of departure is the subject of some debate and not a little confusion. The original Post Office, two sites earlier than the current one in the East End of the town, appears in fact to have been where the current Woolworths' store is, beside the Royal Bank of Scotland. (See p.44) The Post Office then moved nearer the centre of the town at 88 High Street, now the Indian Garden Tandoori Restaurant, opposite what was the Ben Nevis Hotel That was used for many years thereafter as the traditional starting point of the race, and is often now referred to as "the Old Post Office".(See p. 48)

Swan having accomplished his notable feat in 1895, there are no further records of any attempts at timed ascents until two years later when a remarkable individual, Lieut. Col. Spencer Acklom of the Connaught Rangers arrived in Lochaber.

NOTABLE ASCENTS OF BEN NEVIS: Lieutenant Colonel Spencer Acklom, who has no intention of competing for the record ascent and who was not properly equipped for climbing, on Friday last reached the top of the mountain from the base in one hour and fifty-three minutes. On Tuesday, Col. Acklom made another attempt when he climbed and ascended the mountain in 2 hours 58 minutes. The ascent occupied 1 hour 43 minutes, with one minute on the top, and the descent 1 hour 14 minutes, an exceptional performance considering the many disadvantages he had to overcome. The record for the ascent and descent is held by Mr. William Swan, Fort William, who completed the journey in 2 hours 41 minutes by ascending in 1 hour 41 minutes, on top 10 minutes, descent: 50 minutes. Mr. Swan is, however, a young man, while Col. Acklom is fifty-three years of age and had no training and undertook the task in cycling shoes and without a guide. The Colonel, who is a staunch abstainer lately ascended Ben Cruachan twice in three days, taking 1 hour 40 minutes on the first occasion, and twenty minutes less on the second. He has climbed many of the higher ranges in the world and has been at great altitudes in the Himalayas. It must be mentioned that Col. Acklom has seen twenty-eight years army service, 18 of which were spent abroad with 14 in India.

(*The Oban Times*, September 18, 1897)

Spencer Acklom was born in Wexford on January 28, 1844. At the age of 20 he appears in the Regimental Roll of the Connaught Rangers, appointed ensign in the 16th Regiment on June 28, 1864. A glittering military career followed with postings to Mauritius and South Africa. Mentioned in despatches in the London Gazette on February 26, 1878, he was awarded a medal and clasp. Another medal followed during his service in the Afghan War, 1880. He retired from the army on March 1, 1893, to appear in Fort William two years later. He died a widower in Brighton, England on March 15, 1922.

The race to be the fastest man to the top of Ben Nevis had by now gathered a momentum of its own and the record was soon to be challenged by all-comers. By now a medal was at stake and the challenge was being taken up on a regular basis.

ASCENT OF BEN NEVIS

It may seem to most people a remarkable occurrence that the record of 2 hours 41 minutes which was established by Mr. Wm. Swan, Fort William about two years ago, and which has not since been challenged, should at last have been broken by a man nearly 54 years of age, especially when the fact of Mr. Swan's exceptional abilities is borne in mind. He is the representative athlete of the neighbourhood, and on 5 occasions bore off the prize for the cross-country race at Oban games. It appears, however, that Lieut. Col. Acklom, who has followed the military profession (from which he retired about four years ago), has been accustomed to mountaineering and rock climbing since he was a child, and he has just beaten Mr. Swan's record. He cycled to and from the foot of the mountain on Saturday, and made the ascent. His time for the double journey was 2 hours 39 1/2 minutes, the ascent occupying 1 hour 46 minutes, and the descent 53 1/2 minutes. Considering the summit of Ben Nevis is distant seven miles from the Post-Office at Fort William, the Colonel's performance is really remarkable.

(*Inverness Courier*, October 5, 1897)

It is round about this point that the Post Office appears to have moved west along the High Street to number 88, from its original site. Spencer Acklom completed his run "thirteen minutes outside Swan's time", before registering another time of 2 hours 55 minutes referred to as being "from the new Post Office". Gradually, as more and more runners went up the mountain, so the time for the ascent and descent came down:

RECORD ASCENT OF BEN NEVIS:

At 12.30p.m. on Thursday Mr. William MacDonald, a journeyman of twenty-five years of age, who is a member of Leith Gymnasium, started on foot from the Post Office in Fort William to the summit of Ben Nevis for the purpose of endeavouring to beat the best previous record. He started off at a good swinging pace, and reached to top in the incredibly short time of one hour thirty minutes. Asking one of the staff of the Meteorological station to take the time he immediately started back on the homeward journey, and reached Fort William at 2.57p.m., thus accomplishing the double trip in 2 hours 27 minutes and beating the previous record by 28 minutes. It will be remembered that Lieut. Col. Acklom, late of the Connaught Rangers, went up and down the mountain in 2 hours 55 minutes, and not until now has the ascent and descent been done in less time. The latter half was performed in thick mist which makes the accomplishment all the more creditable. To those who have climbed Ben Nevis the present feat will need nothing in the way of commendation, and when it is stated that the Observatory is distant from Fort William seven miles by road and mountain path composed mainly of boulders, the performance will appear almost incredible. Mr. MacDonald on his return was accorded a hearty cheer by the crowd assembled at the Post Office and after being rubbed down was borne through the streets on the shoulders of his companions. He is at present camping on the banks of the Caledonian Canal.

(*The Oban Times*, August 13, 1898)

Mr MacDonald's time was, according to no less than Lt. Col. Spencer Acklom, a "splendid and remarkable one". As to whether he himself would try and lower it, he said: "I dare say yes; I will not say no." In saying that, the worthy Acklom understated his own achievement on his own first run. Having arrived in Fort William, he had set off for the top with no knowledge of what lay before, "with some clothing in a bundle over my shoulder to wear on top." Such was the man's stamina and fitness that he regularly cycled to Inverness and Oban from Fort William. His runs, he said himself, were achieved "casually, without any particular training at all." His view of the challenge was, by definition, completely different from that of Kilgour: "True sportsmen," Acklom opined, "contend for sport, not for reward."

Lt Col Spencer Acklom's success as a hill runner was at the time put down to experience gained in the Himalayas and in India where he served part of his military career. He is pictured here (second left, rear with the sash) at Chaubuttia, India in 1884. Mrs Spencer Acklom is pictured far left in the middle row. Incidentally, the strange item in the centre of the photograph is the "Jingling Johnny" captured by the 88th Connaught Rangers from the French at Salamanca during the Peninsular Wars.

THE BEN NEVIS RECORD: Starting from the Fort William Post Office at 9.00a.m. M. Hunter of Edinburgh reached the Observatory on the summit of Ben Nevis at 10.33a.m., and being rested for four minutes he set off on the return journey. When near the foot of the mountain he unfortunately slipped and inflicted a nasty gash near the kneecap of his left leg. An eager, expectant crowd assembled at the Post Office to welcome the competitor and as time wore on excitement increased. Hunter, however, failed to arrive until 11.35a.m., thus taking two hours thirty minutes to the double journey, which is six minutes in excess of the time occupied by Mr. MacDonald. On the whole the weather was good and well suited for mountaineering, although there were two to three inches of fresh snow on the hill top and for some distance down the slope.

*(**The Oban Times**, September 24, 1898)*

Another run of 2 hours and 20 minutes by Swan on October 29 the same year earned him a new record, and a Gold Medal, which was presented at a special ceremony in the town on a stormy Friday evening, December 23. The medal was donated by Mr John B. Patrick, 8 Woodburn Terrace, Edinburgh. Swan's new time then left him as holder of the records from both the old and new Post Office and the epithet "The Ben Nevis Sprinter".

The occasion at which the medal was presented was a concert organised by Lodge Lochaber of the Loyal Order of Ancient Shepherds. In his acceptance speech, Swan modestly acknowledged the tributes paid to his achievements. The medal was an honour to the town and district, he said, and not a personal one.

In my opinion, if you will allow me to say it, I consider the feats of Colonel Acklom of much greater merit than my performance. I say his record is the best of the two. The Colonel is a truly wonderful man. If my record is beat - which I believe it will be, as all records are made to be broken - if the successful climber will come from the north or from the South, I hope that some of the Lochaber lads will in turn reduce it a little further - (applause). It is my wish that the record should always be kept in Lochaber - (applause). Where also should it be than at the foot of our own mighty Ben? - (applause). I thank you for the reception both tonight and on my return from the Ben, but I would much prefer to try and take another few minutes off the Ben Nevis record than stand up here and try to give a speech - (laughter). I again thank you ladies and gentlemen - (applause).

*(**Fort William News**, Thursday, December 29, 1898)*

The Fort William News, incidentally, also frequently published long lists of the visitors to the hotel and observatory at the top of the Ben. One such visitor, for example, was Dr Jier F. Rudolppen of Berlin, reported on October 13, 1898. The newspaper itself was published for a short period (under two years) at the end of the 1890s.

ASCENT OF BEN NEVIS - A NEW RECORD ESTABLISHED

Starting from the Post Office at 10.30a.m. Mr Swan reached the Observatory on the summit of Ben Nevis at four minutes past noon. Spending one minute there, during which he drank a cup of cold tea and was photographed, Swan again started down the homeward track, arriving at the Post Office at 12.50p.m., thus accomplishing the arduous task in two hours twenty minutes which is seven minutes less than the time occupied by Mr. MacDonald. On his arrival at Fort William, Mr. Swan was greeted with enthusiastic cheering by a large crowd who had assembled and, after being photographed, he was carried shoulder high through the main street of the town. The accomplishment, it may be mentioned, was performed under somewhat adverse weather conditions. Though the air was bright and fine at sea level, Ben Nevis was more or less enveloped in fog while near the top some snow lay on the track. To those who are acquainted with the bridal (sic) path which was followed by the present competitor for nearly the whole distance, the feat will appear almost incredible, and no words of commendation are necessary.

(The Oban Times, November 5, 1898)

The Fort William News of the same weekend reports that Mr MacDonald of Leith had arrived in the town that Tuesday with a view to making an attempt on Swan's record. On being asked whether he thought the record of two hours and twenty minutes would be difficult to reduce, he said: *"No; it won't be difficult to reduce. Of course I would not have come at all were it not that I was sent against my will by the Gymnasium."*

Fifty-four year old Acklom (MacDonald and Swan were both below 30 at the time) was also waiting for better weather to mount another assault on the record and the newspaper said the honour of being the fastest man to the top for the season lay "between these three gentlemen".

Lt. Colonel Spencer Acklom, who had a way with words as well as a hugely interesting lifestyle, meanwhile wrote regarding the Ben Nevis record :

Ben Nevis can hardly be called elegant and picturesque as compared with the two sky-piercing stacks of Ben Cruachan, but it is rougher and more massive, and to my mind can be compared to nothing more appropriately than the body of an elephant. It is situated south east from Fort William and the distance from the Post Office by the roadway or track is fully two and a half miles, and takes fully forty minutes to walk at the rate of four miles an hour. I have paced the distance going and coming as accurately as I can judge, trying the pace on the ground with a measure, and this is what I can make it, although Mr. MacKenzie, who is employed on the road and collects the toll, is of the opinion that it is two and three quarter miles. We will call it two and a half, better under that over. The length of the track from the spring of the hill to the Observatory is five miles so that the total distance from the Post Office to the Observatory is seven and a half miles by the track, or fifteen miles there and back.

(The Oban Times, October 29, 1898)

For all Kilgour's scepticism about the event, he appears to have held the physical achievements of the runners in some regard:

> "Try to imagine what the accomplishment means. Fifteen miles and a "bittock" is the length of the double journey, and to travel this distance on the flat, in the record holder's time, would be no mean feat for an individual; but when one has to contend with boulders on an inclination as steep in parts as 1 in 5, matters assume an entirely different aspect. Not only is this so, but the hill sprinter had frequently to pilot himself out of banks of fog and mist, o'er mountain streams, and through blinding snow showers, while an error in judgement might mean a broken limb or a fractured skull."
>
> *(Twenty Years*, pp46-47)

The enthusiasm now evident for the timed challenge, and the haphazard nature of the bids to beat the time, eventually led to a more formalised attack on the record. It needed to be settled once and for all - the fastest man to the top. On June 3, 1898 the proprietor of the Lochiel Arms Hotel in Banavie, Mr Menzies, offered a Gold Medal to the first man to finish in the race - yet another route, and this time ten competitors ran together. The distance was apparently one mile longer than the course from the new Post Office and was the first to be run under Scottish Amateur Athletic Association rules. The race, involving ten runners, was started (not for the first or last time) to the sound of a shotgun.

Lochiel Arms, Banavie

THE BEN NEVIS RECORD - A LOCAL MAN WINS

Participants in the race were at liberty to ascend the mountain by any route, and after reaching the Observatory, return as quickly as possible to Banavie. Altogether, there were ten competitors who were started at eleven o'clock by Mr. William Lapsley, official timekeeper of the Amateur Athletic Association, Mr. Menzies, the organiser, acting as referee on the summit.

An interested crowd witnessed the start, and followed with their eye the progress of the sprint up the mountainside. Although dull, the weather was otherwise favourable but there was a good deal of snow on the higher reaches of Ben Nevis, as well as the occasional bank of fog, which, doubtless hindered climbers to some extent. Considerable diversity of opinion prevailed as to who the probable winner would be, as those who took part in the race included several well-known athletes and harriers from Edinburgh and other places in the south.

As the time wore on the excitement increased, and the spectators eagerly scanned the hillside for the return of the runners. Shortly after one o'clock one of the competitors was observed coming over the shoulder of Meall An t-suidhe, and this turned out to be Hugh Kennedy, under-keeper at Tor Castle, near Fort William who reached the winning post at 1.43p.m., having performed the double journey in 2 hours 41 minutes. His respective times were: left: 11.20a.m., arrived 12.46p.m., returned to Banavie: 1.43p.m. The next to arrive was William MacDonald, Leith who took thirty two minutes longer than the winner. Kennedy is only twenty-one years of age, strongly built, and of medium height, being descended from a hardy athletic stock.

(The Oban Times, June 10, 1899)

The summit Observatory was still in operation at this time and Hugh Kennedy's arrival at the summit was relayed to the assembled masses at the start by means of a telegram from the summit.

Kilgour - never one to disappoint in this regard - was dismissive of the whole event. The medal which had been offered for "the establishment of an authentic competitive

Lochy Bridge and Ben Nevis, the route taken by Kennedy.

record for the climbing of Ben Nevis" was unceremoniously shot down as "a trinket intrinsically not worth more than a couple of guineas."

"Wherein," Kilgour boomed, "lay the glory and honour if health and strength in consequence are to be permanently impaired, not to speak of danger to limb and life?"

Given the nature of this particular event, and its running under Scottish Amateur Athletic Association Rules, this could arguably be claimed to have been the first Ben Nevis "Race". However, within a few months, by the end of August, Mr MacDonald of Leith, no doubt with a point to prove, had set a new record for the "official course" - 2 hours and 18 minutes.

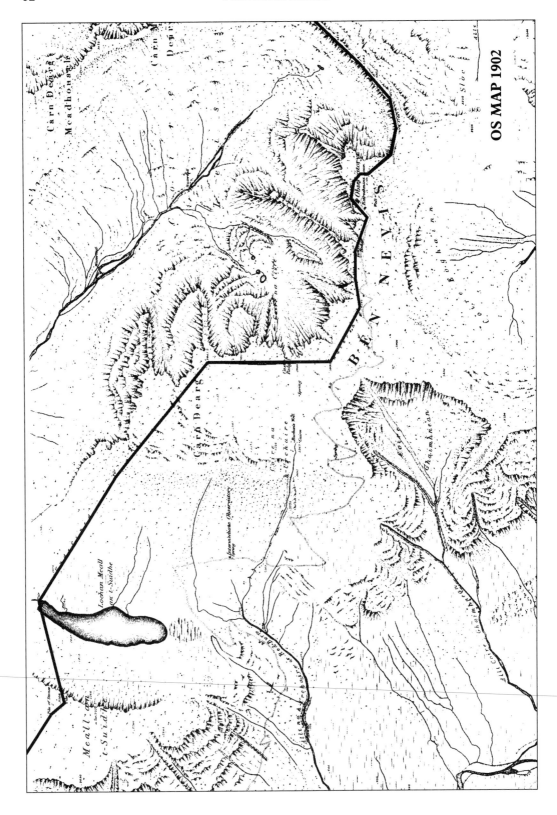

OS MAP 1902

Such was the interest in the Ben at the time, in terms of records, that *The Oban Times* of July 1, 1899, saw fit to detail the current standings:

Up to that point, the best times for the 15 mile run from Fort William itself were:

1895	30 September	W. Swan (Fort William) (27)	2 hours 41 minutes
1897	6 October	Lt. Col. Spencer Acklom (Connaught Rangers) (54)	2 hours 55 minutes
1898	4 August	W. MacDonald (Leith) (25)	2 hours 57 minutes
1898	29 October	W. Swan (Fort William) (30)	2 hours 20 minutes

Twenty-one year old H. Kennedy of Tor Castle was credited with the best time for the 16-mile version of the run from Banavie - 2 hours 41 minutes, completed on June 3, 1899.

Aged Ascents

1899	23 August	Rev. Peter MacBride (Dunoon) (aged 81)
1895	28 June	J. G. Gillespie (Edinburgh) (60)
1895		Adam Galt (Kilbirnie) (76)

The Youngest Ascent recorded at the time was Bella Stewart, aged 3 months, who was carried up in her mother's arms on August 23, 1891.

The Observatory and the Hotel at the top of Ben Nevis.

By the turn of the century the race to the top had become the ultimate sporting challenge and a matter of some pride to the individuals concerned. It was to survive as a race for three more years, and Kilgour was to be vindicated in his carping criticism. Regular attempts, however, were made to beat the best time.

BEN NEVIS RECORD BEATEN: Starting from Fort William Post Office at 8.05a.m. MacDonald reached the summit at 9.34a.m. where he spent a minute drinking a cup of cold tea. Leaving again at 9.35a.m., he put on a good pace on the homeward journey but when near the half-way house he unfortunately tripped and fell amongst a lot of boulders which cut his left arm and thigh. Regaining his footing immediately he continued the sprint down the mountainside, and reached the winning post at 10.23a.m. thus accomplishing the double journey, as already stated, in 2 hour 18 minutes. The winner was accorded a hearty cheer by a large crowd of spectators who had assembled to witness the finish of this somewhat novel race. The day, while not an ideal one for such a performance, was dry and very sultry, and a good deal of fog hung around the upper reaches of the mountain. These adverse weather conditions, however, did not seem to interfere with the competitor's progress to any appreciable extent, and while such a feat must always be attended with considerable danger, it must be conceded that to cover 15 miles, and that chiefly hill climbing, in 2 hours 18 minutes, is, to say the least of it, no mean performance.

(The Oban Times, **August 5, 1899)**

Another Ben Nevis record:

On Monday morning two young fellows named R. W. Cockburn and J. Taylor walked two miles to Edinburgh and caught the early train to Fort William where they arrived at 10.00a.m. After partaking of some light refreshments they made the ascent of Ben Nevis which is presently covered in snow, and stayed a short while with the meteorologists at the Observatory, and returned again to Fort William where they joined the south-going train which leaves for Edinburgh shortly after four o'clock. This is the first known occasion on which anyone has journeyed from the Scottish capital to the summit of Britain's highest mountain and back again in one day. The difficulties of negotiating the ascent of Ben Nevis at this season of the year are legion, and the exploit is therefore all the more creditable.

(The Oban Times, May 24, 1902)

The "gentler sex" as Kilgour sarcastically points out, had up until the turn of the century been barred from the race, (he rather more picturesquely and sourly puts it as having "failed to escape the infection") but in 1902, the inevitable occurred. The first recorded attempt was made by Lucy Cameron (she later became MacDonald) of Glen Mallie (Ardechive). She is understood to have made a reconnaissance of her route the day before her ascent and had walked all the way from Glen Mallie near Banavie, to Fort William the day before that, according to some sources. Her time of 2 hours and 3 minutes, made from the Post Office, was to earn her a handsome gold medal.

Lucy Cameron's medal, by kind permission of Molly Cameron, Inverlochy.

A PLUCKY LADY MOUNTAINEER

On Tuesday morning Miss Lucy Cameron, Glenmallie, made another plucky attempt to reduce the female record for the ascent of Ben Nevis. This unique contest, in which the guerdon is a gold medal, given by Mr. W. Swan, Fort William, has attracted marked attention, and a number have signified their intention of competing. It will be recalled that some time ago Miss Cameron, who is only twenty years of age, made the ascent in 2 hours 17 minutes, but on that occasion the weather conditions were unfavourable. While Tuesday was not ideal for climbing, it was not all together unsuitable with the result that Miss Cameron reduced her previous time by 14 minutes, having accomplished the feat in 2 hours, 3 minutes, being 3.5 minutes in excess of the time occupied by the record holder.

(*The Oban Times,* October 4, 1902)

A further attempt on the ladies' new record was then made by Elizabeth Tait, the post runner at Corrour, on the evening of July 19. Her time of 1 hour 59 minutes and 30 seconds for the ascent, again from the Post Office, was to stand for some time.

A POSTWOMAN'S FEAT

Looking to the prospective closing of the Ben Nevis Observatory and to the fact that no authentic record of female climbers had been established on that mountain, Mr. William Swan, Fort William, himself a well known hill climber, recently signified his intention of presenting a gold medal to the lady competitor who, during the present season, made the ascent of Ben Nevis in the shortest time.

The first competitor in this somewhat novel race started from the Post Office, Fort William, on Saturday morning last at 7.59. a.m., but as only a few knew of the exploit, no crowd assembled to see her off. Her name is Miss Elizabeth Tait, and she follows the occupation of postwoman, traversing the remote glens between Corrour in Perthshire and Lubult in Lochaber. She had thus an excellent opportunity for training for her mountaineering feat. Her performance on Saturday fully justified the confidence placed in her.

Arrangements had been made for telegraphing the time of her arrival at the summit, and a considerable number were not a little surprised to learn, on receipt of the telegram, that the plucky postwoman had accomplished the task in 1 hour 49.5 minutes, reaching the Observatory a minute and a half before ten. This is a remarkable performance for a female climber and will be very difficult to beat.

(The Oban Times, July 26, 1902)

The following year, 1903, was to see two timed races, one involving seven men, which has given us the earliest picture of an organised start. It was run from Achintee farm to the summit only and won by Ewen Mackenzie the Ben Nevis Observatory Roadman. There is unfortunately no record of the time taken although Charles Steel recalled that one or two of Fort William's older citizens in the 1950s believe it to be just over one hour. It was known at the time that MacKenzie had run up the mountain from Achintee in one hour eight minutes.

FORT WILLIAM NEWS: ANOTHER BEN NEVIS MEDAL

Those interested in what has come to be regarded as an annual event, will be pleased to learn that Mr. R. Anderson, jeweller, has signified his intention of offering a handsome gold medal to the competitor who, during the coming season, establishes the best record for a race from the Post Office to the Observatory on Ben Nevis and back. Interest in this somewhat strange competition was strengthened last year by the entry of lady competitors, and doubtless the gentler sex will also be represented in the new contest.

(The Oban Times, March , 1903)

BEN NEVIS RECORD

The syllabus for a new competition for the Ben Nevis record has just been published. The race, to take place on 28th inst., will be from the Post Office at Fort William to the summit of Ben Nevis and back, the prizes to be competed for being a piece of silver plate, timepiece and case of carvers, while a gold medal will be presented to the competitor making the best reduction in the existing record of 2 hours 18 minutes. Mr. J. Brownrigg, Scottish Amateur Athletic Association, Glasgow, will act as starter and time keeper. A goodly number of competitors have already entered for the contest.

(The Oban Times, September 12, 1903)

The race, which started from Achintee and was for the ascent only, was started by Major Cameron, factor to the Cameron Lucy Estate, with a shot-gun. Ewen MacKenzie, the Observatory road-man emerged as the winner, although no record of his time exists. He was one of six Fort William men to take part. The others were D. MacNaughton, W. Riach, the redoubtable Mr. Swan (third from the right), D. Rankine, J. Rankine. the seventh runner was D. Cameron, Tomnaharrich.

There is no record of the date on which the race, was run, but on September 28, Ewen MacKenzie and Hugh Kennedy took part in another race along with a Glasgow runner R. Dobson of Glasgow. The race was the first from the Post Office at 88 High Street. Ewen MacKenzie's winning time of 2 hours 10 minutes 6.8 seconds from the Post Office for the

Ewen MacKenzie on his way to the line in the first official race from the Post Office at 88 High Street, 1903, setting a record.

ascent and descent was to be the last recorded for 34 years. It was to remain undefeated for a further two years after that.

BEN NEVIS CLIMBING RECORD
ACCIDENT TO A COMPETITOR

Interest in the novel contest of ascending Ben Nevis against time was revived on Monday, when a race took place from the Post Office at Fort William to the summit of that mountain and back. In consequence of former records having been flouted in certain athletic and other circles, care was taken on the present occasion to secure the services of an official starter and timekeeper in the person of Mr. J. W. Brownrigg, of the Scottish Amateur Athletic Association, Glasgow, with a view to obtain an authentic and indisputable record of the various times taken. Three competitors took part in the race, namely Ewan Mackenzie, Blarmachfoldach, Fort William; Hugh Kennedy, Achnacarry; and Robert Dobson, a member of the Maryhill Harriers. The day, while somewhat sultry, was otherwise an ideal one for the exploit, and huge crowds of people assembled to witness both the start and the finish of the race. At 12.30 the competitors were started by Mr. Brownrigg at the Post-Office, and the three kept pretty well together till the base of the mountain was reached, where, owing to the narrowness of the path, single file had to be resorted to. Up to the half-way station Mackenzie and Kennedy were not far separated, but at this point the former put on a spurt, and soon outdistanced his companion, Dobson meanwhile being well in the rear. As the respective competitors reached the Observatory at the hill-top, their times were wired up by one of the observers to the official timekeeper, and everything was done to obviate future dubiety. The previous best record for the double journey has for some time been held by MacDonald of Leith, his time being 2 hours 18 minutes, and many surmises were indulged in as to the prospect of this being beaten. By 2.30 large crowds lined the main street of Fort William in anticipation of the arrival of the competitors, and in a short time several cyclists brought the news that Mackenzie was coming. This proved to be correct, and he was soon observed going strong amid the cheering crowd, who gave vent to a loud shout of applause as he reached the goal, almost eight minutes quicker than the time occupied by MacDonald. His different times were:- Ascent, 1 hour 27 minutes; descent, 43 minutes 6 4/5 seconds - total, 2 hours 10 minutes 6 4/5 seconds. Kennedy who arrived second took 2 hours 20 minutes 21 3/5 seconds. Both these competitors, although toil stained by the arduous performances, were quite fit, and after a bath, and a rub down, appeared none the worse of their exploit. The prizes consist of a handsome gold medal, several pieces of silver plate, &, and these were presented in the evening. To the uninitiated such an accomplishment may not appear to be of much moment, but when it is borne in mind that the distance covered is equivalent of 15 miles, and that the average gradient on the mountain is about 1 in 5, some idea of the marvellous nature of the feat will be apparent. To cover the above distance on the flat in the time Mackenzie took would be no mean performance, but when it is a case of avoiding boulders, bogs, and ravine, and piloting one's way through mist, the value of the performance is enhanced. Mackenzie, who is about 30 years of age, is in the employment of the Scottish Meteorological Society as roadman on Ben Nevis. He is over 6 ft. in height, of robust constitution, and from the nature of his calling, was in first-class training for the climb.

Later in the day, Robert Dobson, the Maryhill athlete, was found unconscious on the bridle path by a tourist who was making the ascent of the mountain. This gentleman happily was a naval doctor, attached to the Home Squadron, now lying in Loch Leven, and he used all the available remedies in the restoration of Dobson. He was, however, unable to restore consciousness, and with the aid of some other climbers, who were descending the hill, the victim was carried to the half-way hut, and a message sent to Fort William. A number of willing hands, along with a local doctor, immediately set out for the hut. It was decided, on arrival there, to have the unconscious man conveyed on a stretcher to Fort William, and this was satisfactorily accomplished at a late hour, after Dobson had been for about nine hours on the mountain. Dobson remained unconscious till about two o'clock on Tuesday morning, having been in that state for almost twelve hours. After regaining consciousness, he mentioned to the doctor, who had remained with him overnight, that the last thing he recollected was being blown down by a gust on the hill. Dobson recovered sufficiently to travel South by the 1.10 p.m. train on Tuesday.

(*Inverness Courier,* October 3, 1903)

According to *The Oban Times,* "over-exertion and heart strain" were the main cause of Dobson's predicament, although eventually his "vitality was restored". Notwithstanding the day's events, the presentations for the race were made later in the evening. Dobson himself expressed his thanks to the people of Fort William in a front-page advert in *The Oban Times* a week later:

BEN NEVIS RECORD

I take this opportunity of tendering my sincerest thanks to all those who so ungrudgingly lent their services on BEN NEVIS during the afternoon and evening on 28th ult. and afterwards at Fort William on the occasion of my unfortunate mishap on that mountain.

R. Dobson
Paisley Street, Govan, 3rd October, 1903

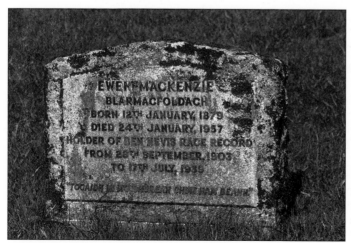

Ewen MacKenzie, true to form as a Ben Race runner, was no average mortal. He once took part in a scientific experiment conducted by the famous Edinburgh physicist Mr J. Y. Buchanan. This appears to have been conducted as part of the first of the two runs up the Ben in 1903.

The aim was to examine MacKenzie's work-rate and the conclusion was that he had generated exactly one-third horse-power over the ascent. He is buried in the Glen Nevis cemetery.

The second of the two races in 1903 was to be the last for some time. The sport "falsely so designated" of running to the top and back again was to stop. Whether it is as a result of the unfortunate Dobson's experience or the closure of the Observatory in 1904, is unclear. Kilgour, as ever, was in no doubt, writing in 1905:

> "While disapproving of the contest, qua such, we of the meteorological staff, as we could not "call it off", interested ourselves in the results and on race days we were all agog with excitement, the man of the night watch even foregoing his quota of sleep to watch the competitors arrive and depart. Now that the Observatory has been shut up, it is very unlikely that any further such contests will be organised, and record breaking on the mountain will be a tale that is told. *Sic transit gloria mundi!*"

(Kilgour, p50)

Kilgour makes no reference though to 82-year old Mr J. Hird from the Uxbridge District, 40 miles from Toronto, who set off to complete the ascent to the top of the Ben just two days before Dobson's race. His effort was described by *The Oban Times* as "extraordinary":

BEN NEVIS
A REMARKABLE CLIMB

Starting form the Lochaber Temperance Hotel, Mr. Hird, accompanied by his son and daughter-in-law, Mr. and Mrs. Hird, went off at a good pace which he maintained along the two miles of county road to the foot of the hill and right up the zig zag path which winds round the shoulder of Mell-an-t-Scoy (sic). Entering the valley of Coire-an L'Urchairean (sic), where the road ascends and is considered the most fatiguing part, he pluckily tackled, and reached the half way hut in two and a half hours time.

After a rest of five minutes Mr. Hird set off again. The path from this point until the summit is reached consists of broken metal, which is most trying but, despite the nature of the road, the climber walked nimbly forward, conversing freely at times and giving expression to his delight at the wonderful panorama of mountain peaks that gradually unfolded to view.

A thousand feet from the summit Mr. Hird encountered snow six inches deep, and while crossing between the plateau just before MacLean's Steep is reached, he was met by blinding showers of snow, but the tall lithe figure which stands six foot pressed determinedly forward, and mastering the last and about the most severe stage of the climb arrived at the Observatory. Having done the journey in 4 hours and thirty minutes the ascent was done in good time, Mr. Hird being none the worse for his exploit and rather proud of his successful achievement. Lumphanans, Deeside, the birthplace of Mr. Hird, will no doubt be proud of one of her sons who left there some sixty-seven years ago with the proverbial shilling in his pocket to push his way to the New World, where he succeeded to a good position in farming.

(The Oban Times, September 26th, 1903)

High Street, looking East, c.1900. The Post Office at 88 High Street is just past the man on the step-ladder on the right hand side.

The next race recorded was to be in 1937, but Mr Kilgour did not have his own way entirely. On September 14, 1909 - (a beautiful autumn morning with a touch of frost), Miss Wilson-Smith of Duns in Berwick-shire made a solo attempt at the race. Starting from the Post Office, she "essayed the hazardous task" on a Tuesday, as *The Oban Times* quaintly put it, and was credited with a time of 1 hour 51 minutes for the ascent. Her time-keeper was none other than William Swan. Four days earlier, she had run from Achintee to the summit in three hours, but as a woman, this was not recognised as a record.

RECORD ASCENT OF BEN NEVIS
LADY'S REMARKABLE RECORD

In the morning when she started off from the Post Office at Fort William she was greeted with loud cheering from an interested crowd of spectators. Setting off at an easy double she reached the base of the mountain in seventeen minutes, and also ran in parts on the bridal (sic) paths. Mr. William Swan, Fort William, who established the first gentleman's record, acted as official timekeeper on the summit and expressed admiration of Miss Wilson-Smith's performance. Seen by our correspondent after her return, the lady was inclined to belittle her so-called feat, and said that she accomplished it at no discomfort to herself. An ardent cyclist, she is in good training, but had only once before made the ascent of Ben Nevis. Her previous highest climb was on the Sidlaws, when she ascended to 2600 ft - only about half of the elevation of Ben Nevis. She underwent no special training for Tuesday's task, and on her return looked as if she might repeat the climb without inconvenience. The day was bright and clear with a touch of frost in the air, and was highly suitable for such an exploit.

(*The Oban Times*, September 18, 1909)

Henry Alexander and his Model "T" Ford in 1911.

FORT WILLIAM NEWS
A DANGEROUS EXPLOIT

An English visitor had a somewhat unenviable experience on Ben Nevis last
week. The gentleman in question has, it seems, earned some notoriety by
scaling hills barefooted and essayed to tackle Ben Nevis in this unorthodox
fashion. When in the vicinity of Claggan he encountered a rustic to whom
he put the question: "Do you think I could climb Ben Nevis in my bare
feet?" Thinking that an attempt was being made 'to get him', the country-
man replied: "Oh, yes, fine that, it's grass all the way." Encouraged by such
an assurance the visitor left his shoes and socks at Claggan, and set off for
the summit unshod. Marvellous to relate he reached the top, but the state of
his feet can readily be imagined by anyone who is acquainted with the rough
bridal path. On reaching the hostelry at the mountain top, he had his gashed
and bleeding extremities bathed and bandaged, and an attempt was made to
manufacture him a pair of wooden dabots. A trial of the home-made sandals
proved, however, their unreliability, and the foolhardy climber had to be
conveyed to Fort William on horseback where his limbs were attended to
medically.

(*The Oban Times*, October 2, 1909)

Interior of Observatory (c. 1903).

The view the runners would have had of the High Street as they headed for the finish line at the original Post Office. The start for William Swan's run in 1895 was where the first group of people are standing on the left hand side, beside what is now the Royal Bank of Scotland. The current Post Office is located on the right on the site of Marshall and Pearson's Garage, (also known locally as "Grant's Garage" after former Provost Duncan Grant).

Chapter 4

1935-45
Modesty and Sportmanship

It is quite possible that there were some timed runs up Ben Nevis in the period between and the years up to and including the Second World War, but no records or reports have survived. The "mania" for getting to the top of Britain's highest mountain, however, clearly continued:

FORT WILLIAM LADY'S RECORD

To return to her native town after an absence of 40 years and climb Ben Nevis in record time is the proud boast of Mrs. Thos. Smith, of Hoo, Surrey. Mrs. Smith, who is 66 years of age, was before her marriage, Miss Christine MacDonald, and for several years was a pupil teacher at the Episcopal School, Fort William. She left Lochaber over forty years ago, and is now paying her first return visit to her native place. Despite her age, she is a keen walker and determined to make the ascent of Ben Nevis before her return home. She set out to walk from Banavie, which is three miles from Fort William, and accomplished the climb to the summit of the Ben in three and a half hours. It is interesting to recall that Mrs. Smith's father, the late Mr. Ian MacDonald, acted as a guide on Ben-Nevis before the construction of the bridle path to the top, and in his day was instrumental in saving the lives of many climbers who had lost their way and were overcome by exhaustion. Mrs. Smith, who looks at least fifteen years younger that her 66 years, claims direct descent from the chiefs of Glencoe.

(*Lochaber News*, Friday, September 25, 1936)

Within a month of Mrs Smith's efforts reaching the attention of the public, timed challenges were once again to the fore, challenges which eventually led to the event's blossoming into a full-blown race with all the organisational back-up that involved and an obviously enthralled populace.

UNSUCCESSFUL ATTEMPT ON BEN NEVIS RECORD

The recent claim by a Tynemouth harrier that he had broken the record for the climb to the summit of Ben Nevis and back, which claim, however, has been hotly contested by Fort William people, who maintain that the starting point was much nearer the base of the mountain than that of the previous holder, seems to have aroused the enthusiasm of climbers throughout the country.

Dan Jack, a young member of the Glasgow Lomond Mountaineering Club, staged an unsuccessful attempt on the record. An interested crowd of spectators, among whom were local people who had watched the start-off of the holder in 1903, assembled at the Fort William Post Office, the recognised starting place for these races, shortly before ten o'clock on Monday morning, and watched the young harrier set off, accompanied by fellow-members of his club. He made quite good time until near the summit of the mountain, when, unfortunately, he strained a muscle in his leg, and had to abandon the attempt. Conditions were ideal for climbing, the bright sunshine being tempered by the tang of frost in the air and but for the unfortunate injury to his leg, it is quite possible that the young climber would have made a bold bid for the record. According to members of the club, attempts will not be discontinued, and it is expected in the near future that other climbers will attempt to better the time of two hours ten minutes set up by Mr. Ewen MacKenzie, the holder of the record, in September 1903.

(*Inverness Courier*, Friday, October 2, 1936)

George Spence, deputy Town Clerk, in running mode.

Within a year, the urge to beat Ewen MacKenzie's time, prompted by the claims of the mysterious "Tynemouth Harrier", had gathered pace. A full-blown race was eventually organised by the Fort William deputy Town Clerk George Spence, himself a mountain climber of some note.

A Challenge Trophy was presented as a prize, by Mr George MacFarlane, who was also to leave his own mark indelibly on the history of the race. He was also eventually to become Provost of Fort William. His sons George and Sandy have given many years of sterling service on the Ben Nevis Race Association Committee.

Conditions for the 1937 race, the first for 34 years, and held on June 28 according to *The Oban Times*, were said to be ideal except for mist at the summit. The starting point was once again the Post Office at 88 High Street.

The 1937 start. C.P Wilson far left, Duncan Cameron and James Martin. The race was in fact then held during the summer months for the next ten occasions, hardly the best conditions for the runners, but near perfect for spectators, who soon took to the event as a spectacle.

Almost an hour before the race was to begin, Fort William High Street, and particularly the area at the Post Office, was crowded with spectators. They had come to see three athletes accepting the challenge of trying to beat Ewen MacKenzie's record of 1903: Charles P. Wilson "an unemployed Kilwinning shipwright", James Watson Martin of Bonnyrigg, a student at Edinburgh University and Duncan Cameron, a gardener employed at Glenfintaig, Spean Bridge. There would seem to be little doubt but that they went further in their preparations for the race than MacKenzie, who is said to have made minimal concessions to getting ready - removing his jacket and tightening his boots!

> As they lined up for the start, Ewen MacKenzie, a 65-year old Kinlochleven factory worker, accompanied the competitors by car to the foot of the mountain and watched them as they made the first part of the ascent. "Wilson had every chance of doing it," he said on his return, "his time to the bend beyond the half-way house was 33 minutes which is a remarkable feat and put him well on the way to break the record."

> On the time being checked, it was found that Wilson's time was 2 hours 17 minutes 52 and 2/5 seconds, as compared to MacKenzie's record of 2 hours 10 minutes 19 seconds.

Interviewed after the race, Wilson appeared quite fresh and felt he could tackle the climb again. "Climbing conditions were ideal," he said, "except at the top, where the mist came down rather suddenly. This rather disconcerted me, and I must have lost between five and seven minutes groping for the path in the thick mist. The path is, of course, terrible, more resembling a river bed in parts, and cannot be compared to what it was in 1903 when it was kept in repair for the transport of goods to the Observatory. It was thoroughly enjoyable and I feel quite fit to do it again."

(*The Oban Times*, July 24, 1937)

1937 winner C.P. Wilson before the start. The man in the hat second from the left is George MacFarlane. Allan Ribbeck, jeweller is to his right and Mr Kennedy, the starter, to his left. The tall gentleman shaking Wilson's hand is believed to be Ewen MacKenzie.

C.P. Wilson was at the time the holder of the record for the Ben Lomond climb. Ewen MacKenzie was enthusiastic in his praise of his achievement. He said: "It was a great attempt and with a little bit of luck he could have succeeded in breaking the record."

The other two runners fared less well. James Martin was almost exhausted when he arrived back at the foot of the mountain and was advised to give up and complete the journey by car. His response, in the spirit of Ben runners for the last one hundred years, was to decline the offer. "I'm going to finish the course, if possible, on foot," he said, carrying gamely on.

He was, however, later found exhausted some distance from Achintee farm by a party of tourists and brought back to the Post Office. He was then "assisted to the manse and given a bath and rub down by members of the committee after which he soon recovered."

Mr Martin, by a remarkable co-incidence, celebrated his 80th birthday on September 1, 1994, just two days before the race. He was at the time visiting Scotland on holiday, having been in Australia for some 20 years. A prior engagement prevented him from attending the race. He is believed to be the oldest surviving runner of a Ben Race at the time of the 1994 race.

George Spence, who checked the times at the summit, reported that Wilson and Martin had made "splendid ascents, there being only thirty seconds between them. Cameron did not arrive at the top and I understand he attempted to take a short cut by striking off the path and making his way over the bracken. This is fatal in a climb of this kind and he had no chance."

C.P. Wilson being borne through the streets after the 1937 race.

Ewen MacKenzie was not the only one to sing the praises of the three competitors. Provost Simon MacDonald, who presented the prizes and the cup, was also suitably impressed. "I did not think the younger generation had it in them."

They did indeed and nine of them (not all of whom were from the younger generation) proved it again a year later on June 28. The day "dawned with lowering skies and as it wore on there were anxious speculations about the weather prospects. Heavy showers were interspersed with gleams of sunshine and heavy mists eddied and rose on the surrounding mountains."

All the hard training done. Duncan MacIntyre relaxes in the sunshine 2 days before the 1951 race.

The race involved an early start for the runners, and indeed the mass of spectators who gathered to the High Street to see them off - 10.30am. Extra police were in fact required to regulate the crowds, many of whom came to see a young man who was entering the Ben Race for the first time, and who was to go on to establish himself as one of the truly great figures of Ben running - Duncan MacIntyre of Fort William.

> **The starters were Charles P. Wilson, Kilwinning, Thomas MacLennan, New Pier, Fort William, Bertram Wilton King, Viewforth Place, Fort William, James Phillip, Dunmure Place, Kilmarnock, Duncan MacIntyre, Butcher, Fort William, Alan Grant, Tomdoun Hotel, Invergarry, David Glen, Croft Tea-rooms, Glen Nevis, Charles P. Dale, Uplawmoor, Glasgow and Phillip Breslin.**

> **Towards 1pm the crowds re-assembled as phone messages had come through from Achintee at the foot of the mountain, reporting the progress of the runners. Tremendous excitement prevailed when it was learned that Wilson was on the level and going strong. He still could not break the record and no-one was more excited than Mr MacKenzie as Wilson appeared along the High Street running strongly. He was given a standing ovation but on comparing stop-watches it was learned that he had just failed to break the record by three and a half minutes. Fresh after his feat, Mr Wilson received the plaudits of the crowd. "It was very treacherous going," he told a reporter, "and the mist swirled and eddied as I was coming down. I fell several times on the slippery surface and rather than wrench my ankle, I slackened off, otherwise I believe I might have done it. However, I will try again. The more I see of Ben Nevis, the more I admire Mr MacKenzie's feat."**

> **Almost as great an ovation was reserved for the second and third men, who are both local; the second being Mr D. MacIntyre, and the third Mr Alan Grant.**

> **The international runner James Phillip, Kilmarnock, experienced very bad luck in the climb. The mist was so thick that he lost the path altogether for a considerable time and was lost."**

> *(The Oban Times, July 2, 1938)*

Wilson, who was forty-one at the time, had set his best time, but was still three minutes outside MacKenzie's record of 1903. Later that month, this time referred to in reports as an "explosives worker", he requested permission to make a solo attempt on the time. The attack was planned for September 17, but in the end postponed. It had been agreed by the race committee that they would take no part in the arrangements and that one day was being set aside for the race every year.

Had Wilson decided to proceed however, and had he broken the record, there was an understanding that it would have been recognised. In the end though he decided not to proceed at this point. "The unsettled state of the weather," he said, "did not justify the risk of bringing officials to Fort William."

And so Ewen MacKenzie's 35 year old record survived, but only for one more year.

C.P. Wilson, on a solo attempt, 1938. He was by now 42 and a father of five children. In desperate running conditions, he failed by just one minute to break MacKenzie's record. "It was better," he said, to ease up, it was so slippery, than risk breaking a leg. It was his third attempt to beat Ewen Mackenzie's historic record.

Sandy MacLaren, proprietor of Star Photos, Perth, at the top of Ben Nevis, winter 1938-39. Runners weren't the only people to get to the top in those days.

A Septenarian's swim and climb

Seventy year old William Tait, retired businessman of Trenton, New Jersey, USA, a native of Fort William, climbed 4406ft. to the top of Ben Nevis in the sweltering heat. The previous day he attempted to swim across Loch Linnhe, but got cramp when he was near the opposite shore owing to the coldness of the water, and had to be taken into the boat that accompanied him.

"I swam nine miles of the Delaware river to prove that a man is not too old at sixty," said Mr Tait, "but the temperature of the water was 30 degrees lower or I would have crossed quite easily." Mr Tait thinks the path up Ben Nevis is much rougher than it was when he last climbed it at the time of Queen Victoria's Jubilee. Near the summit, he said, the path has become dangerously near the edge of the precipice due to the crumbling away of the rock. It is only about five feet away from the edge and in strong wind, which is frequent on the Ben, a person might easily be blown over the edge.

(*The Oban Times*, August 13, 1938)

The 1938 start. C.P. Wilson is far left.

Nine runners again faced the challenge of the Ben at the end of July and Wilson, determined to break MacKenzie's mark, was again amongst the runners. Hundreds of people lined the High Street for the 10.30am start and extra police had to be drafted into the town to keep the way clear for heavy vehicular traffic. There was no by-pass or pedestrianisation in those days!

The nine runners who took part in what was to be an historic race were: Robert Kirk, (Fife); Charles P. Wilson, Kilwinning; James Dale, Glasgow; Duncan MacIntyre, Fort William; Daniel Mulholland and Michael Reavey, both Ardeer Recreation Club; Thomas MacLennan, Fort William; Alan Grant, Invergarry and James Waugh, Glasgow.

> There was little optimism shown that the old record would go as the heavy mist crept down to the very foot of the surrounding mountains. Car parties who followed the competitors and watched with telescopes and field glasses as they made the ascent of the mountain, lost sight of the runners in the thick mist where they were barely a quarter of the way up the mountain. About three quarters of the way up, Mulholland took the lead from Duncan MacIntyre and checked in at the summit a bare ten yards ahead of his work-mate Reavey.
>
> Duncan MacIntyre arrived at the summit a bare half-minute behind, but just as he was making the turn to descend, he slipped and had the bad luck to break his spectacles, the glass of which cut his face.
>
> As the time drew on, the High Street again filled rapidly with spectators who waited anxiously to know whether the record would go. There was thunderous applause as the figure of Mulholland was seen running strongly down the deep lane of people and when it was learned that he had broken the record by nearly seven minutes, he received a tremendous ovation. When Reavey arrived two and a half minutes later, and it was announced that he had also broken the record, the enthusiasm of the spectators knew no bounds.
>
> The arrival of Duncan MacIntyre, the first local competitor, heralded a great burst of applause mixed with commiserations when it was learned of his bad luck. Charles Wilson received the plaudits of the crowd for his modesty and sportsmanship and was loudly cheered when he arrived fourth looking wonderfully fresh apart from a cut where he had fallen. Alan Grant, Tomdoun Hotel, who was fifth, also looked fit and fresh when he arrived two minutes later.
>
> (*The Oban Times*, July 22, 1938)

Wilson's great bid to win a third successive race and break the elusive record failed, ironically to a team-mate from his home club. Daniel Mulholland (who was a well-known cross-country runner and general all-round athlete, finished in two hours, three minutes and forty-three seconds), was at the time employed in Fort William working with Michael Reavey, a native of Strabane in Northern Ireland.

He came home in 2 hours 5 minutes 30 seconds. Duncan MacIntyre recorded 2 hours 12 minutes, an improvement of eleven minutes on his previous attempt.

This was all the more commendable given that conditions for the race, which again started from the Old Post Office, were not good, with mist and heavy going. Mulholland's record, which for a variety of reasons remains unbeaten to this day, was regarded as remarkable. He said after the race: "For most of the way, visibility was no greater than twenty feet and the going was slippery and treacherous. For a good part of the way Reavey and I were both lost and it was just luck that we struck the path. I think under better conditions the record could be lowered further."

The unfortunate Waugh meanwhile had collapsed and was taken to the Belford Hospital but soon recovered.

Reavey was, in fact, completely inexperienced in this type of race and it is almost certain that the two of them (and possibly others) would have lowered the record even further given decent conditions.

That evening, a large crowd gathered at the Town Hall to see the record-breaking Mulholland receive the Challenge Trophy from George MacFarlane. Mulholland and Reavey both received gold watches for breaking the record and Duncan MacIntyre also received a prize.

By now (believed to be 1938 or 1942) the Ben Nevis Race was firmly established as a major local event. It is reported that "hundreds of people travelled to the town from the outlying districts to watch the start and finish and to follow the fortunes of the runners on the hill itself."

Duncan MacIntyre meanwhile was rapidly becoming something of a personality himself. Within a week of coming third in the race, he led a party of what was referred to as "distinguished Scots" as well as Prince Gustav of Sweden, up and down the mountain in misty conditions!

Wall of water on Ben Nevis

A hundred foot wall of water which appeared on the Carn Dearg Ridge of Ben Nevis is engaging the attention of Fort William engineers. The phenomenon was first noticed by Mrs Ross of Lochy Bridge Cottages at 11.00am on Sunday. It had the appearance of a huge fountain, but unlike a fountain, it appeared at regular intervals of ten minutes between eleven o'clock and two o'clock in the afternoon, rising to an estimated height of 100 feet and quickly subsiding.

Mrs Ross, who has lived in the cottage for many years, said this was her first experience of the phenomenon. "I was startled by its appearance," she declared, "and in the general excitement thought Ben Nevis had become volcanic. When I cooled down I realised that it was a water fountain but I could not understand the mystery. I estimate the height of the fountain would be 100 feet and 20 feet wide at the base, but it is difficult to give an accurate account of the distance."

In the afternoon engineers of the British Aluminium Co. climbed the ridge where the waterfall was to be seen. Near the ridge are the five pipes which convey the waters of Loch Treig through the Ben Nevis tunnel to the British Aluminium Power House at Fort William. It is believed the phenomenon may be caused by an airlock at one of the intakes to the tunnel.

(*The Oban Times*, **August 5, 1939**)

The 1939 start and the record was finally broken. The terrier did not run!

Events elsewhere in Europe conspired to halt the race for a time, but not for long. There were no races in 1940 or 1941, but on Wednesday May 20, 1942, at 5pm, a record entry of eleven runners, including record holder Daniel Mulholland and C. P. Wilson, set off from the Post Office, with the revived race forming the highlight of "Warship Week".

The runners who set off and the crowd who waited patiently at the finish on the High Street were unaware of the drama which was to unfold in the next two and a half hours. It was to rank, in sporting terms at least, with the most tragic of moments, as Duncan MacIntyre ("Duncan the Butcher"), who had finished third three years earlier, led the race with a hundred yards to go.

And just as Dorando Pietri collapsed near the end of the 1908 Olympic marathon in London and Jim Peters was to do famously at the Commonwealth Games in Canada in 1954, so the unfortunate Duncan was overcome with the finish line and victory in sight. He was, unfortunately for him in terms of winning the challenge, helped by his brother Alister and therefore disqualified.

Hugh MacLeod, a young policeman in Fort William at the time, delighted with his progress and surprised that he had done so well, coasted towards the finish oblivious of the fact that his great friend had succumbed to exhaustion. It was Hugh's first Ben race, having been persuaded by Duncan MacIntyre and Jock Petrie to take part.

The shock of realising that Duncan had failed to finish in such tragic circumstances made a lasting impression on Hugh. His recollection of the day's events remain crystal clear in his 77th year. "It was a devastating blow to realise that my good friend Duncan had fallen so close to the line. Of course I didn't know that at the time, and I just kept going at my own pace. But it was such a wonderful thing that he went on to win the race the following year. I think everyone wanted him to do that after what happened. But yes it was a terrible way to finish after such a great effort."

Six of the eleven runners finished officially, with Wilson of Kilwinning, improving on his fourth place in 1939, to win the event, albeit in most fortuitous circumstances. It was his third win since 1937. It wasn't to be his last either, as he continued to distinguish himself as an athlete of the highest class.

> **There was much excitement as one of the competitors was seen at the east end of the High Street running strongly. The cheering swelled to a roar when it was ascertained that this was Duncan MacIntyre, and although it was by now quite definite that he would not break the record, his expected win was a popular one. When Duncan arrived about 50 yards from the tape he was seen to falter and then collapse on the roadway. Immediately, a doctor was summoned and as he was being tended, C. P. Wilson shot past him and went on to finish in a time of 2 hours 25 minutes 49 seconds. Next in was Constable MacLeod eight minutes later and he was followed by Lieut. Gowans whose time was 2 hours 40 minutes 10 seconds. Mulholland, the record holder, was overcome by cramp and came in fourth.**
>
> **(The Oban Times, May 30, 1942)**

1942 RACE RECORD

1   C. P Wilson,
Kilwinning
        2 hours 25 mins 49 secs

2   Hugh MacLeod,
Fort William
        2 hours 33 mins 03 secs

3   Lieut. Gowans, R.N.
HMS St Christopher
        2 hours 40 mins 19 secs

4   L/Cpl Meldrum
        2 hours 48 mins

5   Jock MacCallum,
Fort William
        3 hours 2 minutes

6   Jock Petrie,
Fort William
        No time recorded.

Three other runners were
listed as starters -

Cpl J. Thomson,
J. Andrews,
J. A. Andrews.
D. Mulholland and
Duncan MacIntyre
both retired.

The 1942 runners. Bottom picture: (runners from left) D. MacIntyre, D. Mulholland, H. MacLeod, Jock MacAllum, Jock Petrie, Lieut. Gowans. C.P Wilson is third from the left in the top picture with George MacFarlane immediately behind him.

Later that evening, the drama which had marked the end of the race was over-taken by the usual frivolities and celebrations. At a meeting presided over by Sheriff Cassells, the prizes were handed over by George MacFarlane. C.P Wilson received a canteen of cutlery and a silver medal; Hugh MacLeod a silver salver still used as a cake stand and a silver medal, and Lieut.Gowans a silver medal. The unfortunate Duncan MacIntyre received a silver medal and special prize for his heroic effort. Mulholland was presented with a vase of Goss china, inscribed with the Fort William coat of arms as a memento. Two prominent speakers were then introduced - the Rt. Hon. J. J. Westwood, Under-Secretary of State for Scotland and Neil MacLean, MP for Govan.

The 1942 race was the first in which servicemen who were training in the area during the war appeared. And to many, the Race was just one of the ways of deflecting the sorry events elsewhere in Europe from the consciousness.

At least 112 Fort William men perished in the First World War. However, in many respects, the Second World War may not have been so hard on the area. It is reported that 24 of the Fort's finest made the supreme sacrifice and returned to Lochaber no more.

Hugh MacLeod's medal

"Thursday evening was passed enjoyably at a successful dance in the Masonic Hall. Gardener's orchestra provided the music and dancers thoroughly enjoyed themselves."

Farewell to Lochaber, and farewell my Jean,

Where heartsome with thee I've mony day been;

For Lochaber no more, Lochaber no more,

I'll maybe return to Lochaber no more,

These tears that I shed, are a' for my dear,

And no for the dangers attending on weir,

Tho' borne on rough seas to a far bloody shore,

Maybe to return to Lochaber no more.

The effects of the war were there for all to see, however. Troops arrived in Lochaber. Light and heavy anti-aircraft batteries were set up to protect the nearby aluminium works. But some effects were kept well out of sight.

Training took place at Loch Eil. The Independent Companies emerged and before long they were called Commandos, living at Achnacarry Castle and Torcastle, undergoing training that was fierce, vigorous and realistic. As Walter Cameron detailed in his history of Fort William, the war years had their lighter moments:

"There was the crofter's wife who found her cows had been bewitched and gave no milk one morning, after the Commandos had been on a "living on the country" exercise in the neighbourhood. The Caledonian canal became the southern limit of a Protected Area, a "Land o' Stay Oot" somebody named it, and military posts were established on the roads "at which all passports were checked". Rumours circulated about mysterious training in remote and hidden places....

The Royal Navy set up a centre within Fort William called St Christopher "for training men in operating small craft" ..... Bombs did fall from time to time. One direct hit was scored by a bomb which landed on the floor of the power house and did not explode. On another raid bombs were dropped in the River Lochy and very close to the farmhouse, now the British Aluminium Company's Lochaber Club."

And so it was in 1943 that the Ben Nevis Race moved to what many regard as its spiritual home - the King George V Park near the Craigs burial ground. The King George as it was affectionately known, (it was referred to as a "bonnie wee thing" by Sir Stewart MacPherson at a Camanachd Association AGM in the 1930s), was surely one of the most spectacular sporting venues in the country, a natural sloping amphitheatre which saw many historic and dramatic sporting events - the Ben Race itself, three Camanachd Cup finals, football matches and Highland Games.

Sporting events in Fort William had centred on the Public Park from 1887 - the piece of ground which was eventually to become known as the King George V Park. Football, shinty and hockey were all played on the lush turf which was gifted to the town by Mrs Cameron Campbell of Monzie, the Superior of Fort William at the time, for use as a public park in commemoration of Queen Victoria's Jubilee. It was officially opened in 1878 and was consequently named Victoria Park.

The King George - to many, still the spiritual home of the Ben Race.

The surface of Victoria Park, in the shadow of the Cow Hill, was said to be "somewhat rough and uneven, just as Nature made it", and it was not until 1936 that extensive alterations were made to the park. Drainage was laid, the surface was levelled and re-turfed and when the work was completed, the name was changed to King George V Public Park.

Keen Sports at Fort William

It was very appropriate that the historic Lochaber gathering should be the first event staged at the reconstructed Victoria Park, Fort William, which has been closed for play during the winter. At an expenditure of abut £2,000 the Fort William Town Council have enlarged and levelled off the field, which is beautifully situated in a sylvan setting of sombre pines, and overshadowed by the historic Sugarloaf Hill. The seating accommodation has been greatly extended, and the new terracing is proving a great boon to spectators. Sir D. W. Cameron of Locheil presided over the gathering, which was largely attended by county families and shooting tenants in the district. The morning dawned dull and cloudy, with a decided threat of rain, but during the forenoon the sun broke through, and a light breeze dispersed the threatening clouds. An innovation which proved of great interest was the hill race, where competitors had to cross boggy country and ascend the Cow Hill which lies behind the park The event was won by P. Kenny, Wishaw, in 14 minutes 23 seconds.

(*Inverness Courier*, August 27, 1937)

The main sporting event held on the field was the Lochaber Gathering, which continued until 1954. The games were followed for a period by the Caol Highland Games. The last sports' gathering which took place there was in August 1969, when the ground was acquired for a new swimming pool, after much angst in the town.

Ironically, the part of the pitch given over to a bowling green has now been returned to its former status as a playing field. Young players from Fort William still use the "Town end" of the park for their shinty practices.

And shinty had figured largely in the life of the aforementioned "Duncan the Butcher" who was to make 1943 his very own year in running terms, albeit that he made a marvellous contribution to the Ben Race as an institution for many years thereafter. He was, indeed, eventually to become President of the Ben Race Association.

Duncan was a remarkable character. He lost an eye in a shinty match in 1934 in an incident with a Ballachulish player who was banned *sine die*. Duncan "the popular half-back" was hospitalised first of all in the Belford and then the Glasgow Eye Infirmary. His predicament however did not stop him going on to set a record of 2 hours 4 mins and 30 seconds when he led home a field of eight runners in 1943.

Fort William shinty Club -1946-47. Duncan, pictured here far right, rear, often referred to his OBE, *"one bloody eye"*. He was also well known for his attempts to beat smoking and was often seen running around drawing on a fake cigarette in his bid to beat the weed.

Conditions for the historic 1943 race, run as the highlight of "Wings for Victory Week" were wet and cold with a few intervals of sunshine, par for the course really given some of the conditions which prevailed over the years. The race was still being run in early summer though - on June 23, and it was only in 1955 that the first weekend of September was settled on as a regular starting point.

Duncan MacIntyre with his winner's trophy. There was no mistaking Duncan's triumph on this occasion , and there were no fatal slips before the line. He led home Daniel Mulholland of Ardeer (on the right) by four and a half minutes with Jock MacCallum (left) of Inverlochy third in 2 hours 17 mins and 40 secs. Duncan's time, a new record from the new start, was to stand for eight years.

Excitement mounted steadily and as one of the runners could be seen rounding the corner at the Belford Hospital there was speculation as to who it could be. There was a tremendous burst of cheering when it was seen that it was thirty-five year old Duncan MacIntyre, a local butcher, who is a regular entrant in the Ben Nevis Race and who last year had the race in his grasp when he collapsed a few hundred yards from home. MacIntyre ran strongly to the tape and, although mud-stained and bleeding from cuts to his arm, was seen to be perfectly fresh. His time was two hours four minutes and thirty seconds. The cheers of the crowd had hardly subsided when another runner appeared. This was Daniel Mulholland of Ardeer Recreation Club, who holds the record for the Old Post Office Race. His time was two hours and eight minutes for the new course. The third man was J. MacCallum Fort William, with a time of two hours seventeen minutes and forty seconds.

(*The Oban Times*, July 6, 1943)

The by now legendary Wilson of Kilwinning came fourth in 2 hours 25 mins and Jock Petrie was fifth, time unrecorded. Three others took part - L/Cpl Pape, Mr Ritchie and Mr Mullin.

The 1944 runners at the King George V Park.

But there was no stopping Wilson. A year later, aged 47, he took his fourth title, winning in 2 hours 14 minutes and 19 seconds, with Mulholland second nearly a minute behind him. Duncan MacIntyre was third in 2 hours 15 mins 50 secs, with Jock MacAllum and Jock Petrie thereafter. Hugh MacLeod and Messrs Hicks, Mullin and Bellinghurst also took part (Hugh Macleod in order to secure a spell of leave from the RAF!). Conditions were very hot on this occasion and it is reported that communications were by the Home Guard.

D. Mulholland (above) heading for the line, in second place, 1944 and D. Mulholland with Duncan MacIntyre (below), 1943.

The 1944 race was to be the last for another seven years as events elsewhere took their toll in more ways than one. The Ben Race though was about to enter a new era and a whole new dawn, and set of competitors, beckoned. The next decade was to be quite simply, the event's Golden Era.

All set to go, 1944. From the left: unknown, C.P. Wilson, (Mr MacFarlane to the rear), D. Mulholland, D. MacIntyre, J. Petrie, J. McCallum, unknown.

Many of the photographs on the proceeding pages were taken by George MacFarlane, who used to have them developed and on display before all the runners had finished.

A Peace Cairn was inaugurated at the top of Ben Nevis in 1945 by Bert Bissell of Dudley, who had first climbed the Ben seven years earlier. Since then, pictured here at the age of 90, Mr Bissell has climbed Ben Nevis more than 100 times. The relationship between Fort William and Dudley in Worcester has gone from strength to strength as Mr Bissell's number of climbs rose. Co-incidentally, the 50th anniversary of the cairn's inauguration, 1995, is also the 100th anniversary of William Swan's first timed run up Ben Nevis.

In 1958 and 1959 The City of Glasgow Police Pipe Band piped the runners to the start, entertained the huge crowds and piped the leading runners home.   *Jimmy Dunlevy*

Chapter 5

1950 -1960
The Golden Era

"While the challenge of Ben Nevis is there forever to see, these men and their many friends must surely have been the inspiration in starting off this new era of mountain running."

(**Eddie Campbell**)

When it was learned that because of the condition of the Town Park, and the general apathy on the part of the public, that the Lochaber Games would not be held this year, a move was made to revive the Ben Nevis Race, which before the war always aroused widespread interest in Lochaber and elsewhere. Under the vigorous leadership of Provost MacFarlane, a committee was formed, and preliminary arrangements were made.

It is hoped to hold the race sometime during the first week in September and the start and finish to return to the original spot.

Full details will be advertised shortly and it is hoped that the response will be as big as it was before the war.

(***The Oban Times***, **July 1, 1950**)

It would appear that "the desired response" was not, in fact, big enough and there is no trace of any further developments in terms of staging a race in 1950. Apathy may indeed have been the main factor in the non-appearance of the race for another year, but the less than delightful Lochaber weather may also have had something to do with it.

The summer was described, as it often is, as being the "worst in living memory", with 3.24 inches of rain falling between Sunday, September 3 and Saturday, September 9 - 1.24 inches of it fell on the Wednesday! The situation was so bad, in fact, that the road between Mallaig and Fort William was blocked near Glenfinnan that day for twenty-four hours.

The race up Ben Nevis due to be run on August 15 is attracting increasing attention. In addition to ten local runners, entries have been received from Inverness, Northern Ireland, Ardlui, Corrour and Glasgow. These entries include one from the junior cross-country champion of Scotland.

Among local entries are Duncan MacIntyre, John ("Jock") Petrie whose enthusiasm and love of the event inspired the committee to carry on and make it one of the highlights of the athletic year.

99

The race will start and finish in the Town Park directly after the official opening of civic week by Provost MacFarlane at 2.45pm. Walkie-talkie equipment will be placed on the summit, at the half-way hut, at Achintee and in the Park itself, so that a running commentary will help everyone follow the runners. ...

Lest any be nervous, it may be said that the whole route will be patrolled by experienced climbers and care will be taken that those who fall by the wayside will be brought down in comfort.

(*The Oban Times*, **August 11, 1951**)

The 1951 start. Eddie Campbell is second from the right.

In addition to the MacFarlane Cup, which was to be presented to the winner of the resurrected race, over £60 in donations and other prizes had been gathered by merchants, hoteliers and citizens of the burgh. Entries were invited up until five days before the race and the start eventually saw 21 competitors renew the challenge.

The events of that Wednesday afternoon in August (it was a 3pm start) and the races which followed in the next ten years or so, spawned what is regarded by many as the Golden Era of the Ben Race.

The fifties also saw the emergence of four local people in particular who established themselves as legends in their own lifetime, with their own very special place in the history of the race and Lochaber - Eddie Campbell, Brian Kearney, Jimmy Conn and Kathleen Connochie (now MacPherson). They were to follow on in the best of traditions as laid down by people like C.P. Wilson, Daniel Mulholland and Duncan MacIntyre.

And so on Wednesday, August 15 at 1pm, 21 competitors lined up at the King George V Park in dry, warm conditions. (There had been some discussion at the Town Council at the beginning of August as to whether bye-laws should be enacted to enable the race to be started at the Post Office, but this was eventually set aside). There was light mist on the summit and Fort William Police and B Company 4/5 Cameron Highlanders Territorials provided the communications and have been involved ever since, as coverage of the event became ever more sophisticated.

Duncan MacIntyre was still there as a new generation of Lochaber runners set off, as was the great figure of Jock Petrie, accompanied by his two sons Charlie and Allan. From Tomdoun came Allan Grant, another previous runner - teenagers and men.

A crowd estimated by *The Oban Times* to be in the region of 2,000 - amongst them the great C. P. Wilson of Kilwinning - saw former Provost George MacFarlane set the challengers off on the race for his own trophy and a new record eventually claimed. Wilson in fact was called on by Major Hume of the organising committee to say a few words before the runners set off. Had he had more warning of the race, he would, he said, have "been glad to have a go" - despite the fact that he was now 53 and a grandfather!

Twenty-one runners set off and it was a twenty-one year old who won, Lochaber's own Brian Kearney in a stunning 1 hour 51 minutes and 18 seconds. It was the first time the elusive barrier of two hours had been broken.

Rear (Left to right): Eddie Campbell, Brian Kearney, Tommy Kearney, Jock Petrie, Charlie Sim, Duncan MacIntyre, Archie MacLachlan.
Front: Alec "Wallace" MacDonald, Allan MacLean, Charlie Petrie, Allan Petrie, Allan Grant, M. Reavie.

Brian Kearney in the lead, 1951

George MacFarlane also presented the prizes including the winner's trophy. Brian Kearney, a local tradesman, received the cup, a gold medal and a prize valued £10 for his efforts. "On the downward trip you have to be careful not to run too fast at first. Your body has to adjust itself to a checking stride which puts a tremendous strain on the leg muscles, and you can't afford to go hell for leather... When the road stretch is reached, runners often find it difficult to adapt to running on level tarmac for the last couple of miles to the finishing post." The "Sydie Map" was used to guide runners on their way, and still is.

The crowd surged to the ropes when it was announced that Brian Kearney, Eddie Campbell and Tommy Kearney had passed Claggan and shortly afterwards the first runner appeared past the hospital, making excellent time. Cheers rang out as Brian Kearney came through the gates of the park and this rose to a thunderous welcome when it was learned that his time was 1 hour 51 minutes 18 seconds, a record for the Town Park Start.

(*The Oban Times*, August 18, 1951)

Brian Kearney

Eighteen-year old Eddie Campbell, who was to dominate the next six years with Brian (only P. Moy of Vale of Leven broke their grip on the race in 1956) received a silver medal and a prize valued at £7 for his second place (1hour 56 mins 35 secs) and Tommy Kearney (Brian's older brother) came in third in 2 hours 9 mins and 18 seconds. In fourth place was none other than 42-year old Duncan MacIntyre, the 1943 record-breaker in a time of 2 hours 10 minutes and 55 seconds.

Another great ovation was reserved for Jock Petrie (48) who completed the course within three hours and qualified for a bronze medal. He was also to take home the silver rose bowl donated by Mrs Evelyn Hobbs of Inverlochy Castle for the oldest competitor in the race.

Brian in fact led to the top of the Ben, arriving in 1 hour 10 minutes, 3 minutes and 30 seconds ahead of Eddie Campbell. All the others finishing the race received bronze medals with their names and times inscribed on them. Runners also received certificates with their times on them.

Lochaber AAC inaugural table meeting.

C. Sim, A. MacKenzie and T. Kearney who finished third, on the assent, 1951

The Herald

The next race, once again in June (on Wednesday 18th at 3pm) in 1952, also saw the introduction of a new trophy, presented to the best team, by Mrs Hobbs. Duncan MacIntyre had by now been elevated to the status of starter and he set 24 competitors on their way, amongst them a contingent from Glasgow and a Skye-man, Murdo Nicholson of Portree. Lochailort's own Farquhar MacRae, better known perhaps in modern times for his fiddling, was running for the second time.

June it may have been, but Ben Nevis was at its most fickle, with a blizzard on the summit. There were 24 starters out of a record 34 entrants and 12 were to finish within the new two and a half hour mark to qualify for the bronze medal. Only the first two home, however, beat the elusive two hour mark.

The winner, in what was regarded as a "remarkably fast time" of 1 hour 53 minutes and 46 seconds, was Eddie Campbell, who led home Charles Petrie (1 hour 55 minutes and 45 seconds). Third was Jimmy Conn in 2 hours and 8 minutes. The second and third placed runners were members of the Ben Nevis Athletic Club and their efforts along with the sixth place of Charlie's brother Allan (2 hours 14 minutes) won them the new team trophy.

**The tartan terrors - Jimmy Conn (centre) and the
Petries, Charlie and Allan.**

For all that only the first two broke the two hour barrier, the finishing times were regarded as commendable given that it had rained all day. Eddie Campbell was later to describe conditions as atrocious with a blizzard at the summit, the worst he had experienced. The new strip worn by the team winners - tartan sleeved shirt and tartan shorts - proved ideal in the wintry conditions which forced nine runners to retire. The use of a large board at the field had enabled the watching crowd to monitor the runners' progress as the misty conditions made visibility poor throughout the day.

St Mary's Fort William (Eddie Campbell, A. Roberts and A. MacLean) were second in the team competition with Inverness Harriers third, R.M.S.V.R. Govan fourth and Glasgow and District 'A' fifth.

The British Legion Pipe Band entertained the assembled crowd however, with Molly Cameron's Highland dancing troupe braving the elements and Highland athletes Ewan Cameron, Lochearnhead and Louis Stewart of Annat adding to the excitement. Molly Cameron was of course a niece of the famous Lucy Cameron of Glenmallie who made a name for herself in 1902.

And the excitement was not confined to the Town Park with a record crowd attending the after-race celebrations in the Town Hall Square, the prizes being handed over by Mrs MacDonald, wife of the vice-president of the Race Committee. All the medals for the 1952 event were, in fact, donated by Jock Petrie. Mrs Hobbs attended, to hand over her own new prize and Miss Marie Manley presented bouquets to both Mrs MacDonald and Mrs Hobbs, who was for many years a faithful supporter of the Ben race.

The Race committee, meeting on July 15, fixed June 24 as the provisional date for the 1952 race. It was decided that the whole course would be clearly marked for the use of those competitors not familiar with the route and the date was to be entered in the Scottish Tourist Board's Handbook. It was also decided that a dinner would be held after the race for competitors, the Press, Committee members and their wives. The Committee even elected an entertainments sub-committee with George MacPherson the secretary and Duncan MacIntyre as his assistant.

1953 start

The 1953 race was eventually run on Saturday July 25 with a 4.30pm start. All competitors were insured during the race, covering a weekly amount of £6 per week for 6 weeks, as along as a medical certificate was obtained. That insurance presumably didn't cover the actions of the starter Jock Petrie, who did the necessary with a double barrel shotgun "which all the runners made sure he was pointing upwards", according to Eddie Campbell. (Mr Petrie's two sons Charlie and Allan both ran the race and finished in the first ten.)

Twenty runners started the race in poor conditions with the Ben visible "on and off". There was even a 100 yard patch of snow to run through at the summit.

It had been poor weather all week, but this had failed to dampen the spirits of the large crowd which gathered in the Town park and along the road. The later starting time had been agreed to let staff and shop-keepers, many of whom had donated prizes, see the race finish.

The Lovat Scouts under Captain Charles W. S. Steel furnished a running commentary of the race. It was heard by the crowd in the park as well as in Glen Nevis and in the village of Inverlochy. Installation of the sophisticated reporting system had been made easier as Cameron of Lochiel had supplied hill ponies to carry the equipment to the top with two keepers John Stewart of Achdalieu and W. MacKay of Bunarbaig taking charge of them.

There were great expectations that Eddie Campbell would break Brian Kearney's record (01.51.18) but in the end he did not quite make it, beating his own time of the previous year by 28 seconds to record one hour fifty-three minutes and eighteen seconds.

The only runner to break the magical two hour barrier, he received a great reception from the crowd all the way from Nevis Bridge to the Town Park and "dozens of small boys padded along at his heels." He was piped home by the Fort William British Legion Pipe band, who were doing the honours for the third time.

D. I. Dando of Lochaber Sports Club came in second (02.00.25) with A. Fleming of Cambuslang Harriers third (02.03.53).

Ten of the runners qualified for bronze medals, finishing in under two hours and twenty minutes. The team prize went to the Ben Nevis Athletic Team who made up the Lochaber Sports Club - Campbell, Dando and Simpson with Ben Nevis - Conn, Charlie Petrie and MacDonald second and Glasgow and District third.

For all the foul weather, there were no casualties and the usual festivities ensued in the evening with Mrs MacFarlane and Mrs Hobbs presenting the prizes.

1953 committee: Chairman G. MacFarlane; Messrs H. Fraser, W. Kennedy, A. MacDonald, G. MacPherson, J. MacPherson, D. MacIntyre, H.V. Manley, J. Petrie, A. Ribbeck, C. W. S. Steel, W. Stewart, J. Thomson.

The committee had been disappointed with the fall in the number of runners, but they resolved to carry on until next year in the hope that interest would pick up again. They were rewarded with better weather, a big crowd, and a new record.

1954 - the runners head for Glen Nevis   *The Herald*

Interest in deeds on the Ben may in fact have been helped by events other than the race itself. In "Operation Benfire" a gigantic beacon was lit at the summit to mark the coronation of Queen Elizabeth. (Over 100 years earlier in 1842 a similar bonfire had been lit to mark Queen Victoria's first tour of Scotland).

The 4.30pm start was repeated for the 1954 race which took place on Saturday, June 26 with Major Hume setting 24 runners (who had paid a two shillings entry fee; 34 had in fact entered) on their way in dry conditions. There was mist, and for the second successive year, unseasonal snow on the summit. Only four failed to finish however.

For those watching and waiting in the King George V Park, there was shinty, football and Highland Games.

This time, five runners broke the two hours with Brian Kearney leading them home in a new record time of one hour forty-seven minutes and four seconds. Eddie Campbell, winner in 1952 and 1953, broke the 1951 record coming home two minutes and five seconds behind Kearney (his fastest time to date) with W. Gallacher of Glasgow a further five minutes behind.

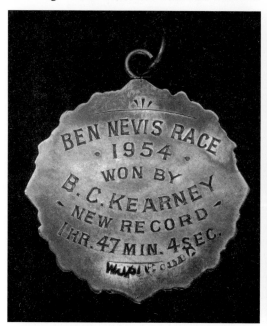 

No less than six of the first eight runners were local, with Brian Kearney's brother Tommy coming home in eighth place.

Brian Kearney, Jimmy Conn and D. I. Dando, with three out of the first four places, not surprisingly took the team prize, running as St Mary's.

Brian's feat in winning the race with a record time was put down to the training he had done working as a bricklayer up at Lundavra, running the seven miles to and from town in his training runs which started in March. He also apparently used "a special stamina restorer" during the race and took one Glucose tablet before starting off!

And on finishing the runners were, for the third year, entertained to high teas in K.K. Cameron's tea-rooms. There was general agreement that Saturday was the best day for the race, although the late finish by slower runners was now giving rise to concern. Even allowing for three hours, it could be 10pm before the summit party returned to base in the event of an accident.

Kathleen Connochie training with Duncan MacIntyre, Corrie Sutherland, Charlie Steel and his nephew.

By 1955, just four years after the Race was set on a sound organisational footing by the BNRA, the event had become one of the country's outstanding marathon events and sporting challenges. The Ben Nevis Race Association was formed with George MacFarlane (father of the current Secretary, George) as President. George MacPherson was in the Chair with Duncan MacIntyre acting as his vice-chairman.

An eleven-strong committee along with Treasurer Charles Steel looked after the event which, affiliated to the Scottish Amateur Athletic Association, attracted over two thousand spectators. Twenty seven runners started the race under the direction of J. Thomson at the earlier time of 3.30pm and just one failed to finish. But there was much more to Saturday, September 3, 1955 than that.

It all started simply enough according to Kathleen herself. No stranger to the race given her father's involvement as a medical adviser, and having the bold Duncan MacIntyre as a family friend, it was perhaps inevitable that she would take part in what was to be a ground-breaking run, which would see her appear not only in the Guinness Book of records but, much to her mother's horror, the *News of the World!*

"We were all sitting in the house one evening just about three weeks before the Race itself and talk was as ever about the arrangements. For no apparent reason, Duncan said to me: "Do you think you could run the Ben race yourself?" I said "I don't see why not!" Dad said: "Of course". Duncan said, "I'll train you", and it started from there."

The rest, as they say, is history. For the next three weeks, Kathleen and Duncan trained in secret on the peat track at the back of Fort William, in the forests between Torlundy and Leanachan and up and down the Ben itself.

As race day approached, Kathleen, who had swum Loch Linnhe in the first of a series of resurrected races along with Jock Petrie amongst others (in 1952 when aged 13), soon became the focus of attention.

Kathleen soon assumed super-star status amongst her school-mates who were, she says, very supportive. "I didn't want people to know that I was running, so a lot of our training was done in secret. But in a place like Fort William, that can only go on for so long."

But the whole plan nearly foundered on the Scottish Amateur Athletic Association's bureaucratic machinations. Word arrived before lunch-time that Kathleen was being forbidden to run. Duncan MacIntyre was furious and withdrew from the race. A local outcry was in the offing. An approach was made to the Ben Race committee and they agreed to make the race facilities available to Kathleen who was to set off two minutes after the main body of runners.

Kathleen Connochie, September 3, 1955. "I'll never forget it."

The day itself was dry with a light wind. There was mist, but no snow on the summit. Then one runner who failed to finish, G. Calder, managed to lose his way in the mist after half-way and did not reach the summit. He was roundly "ticked off" for not reporting to the nearest official.

His predicament however failed to divert attention from the two highlights of the day - Eddie Campbell's fine win in one hour fifty minutes and five seconds and Kathleen Connochie's dramatic three hours and two minutes, establishing a women's record which to this day remains unbeaten. The qualification for the bronze medal had incidentally now come down to two hours and fifteen minutes.

Kathleen Connochie's run was unforgettable in many respects. She herself will never forget the surge of adrenalin as she approached the field. "I felt really fresh and we had had a great time coming down the hill. At one stage Duncan disappeared to go and wash himself having fallen in a bog and I know there was consternation in the field when it was announced that we had been separated. Then we passed the SAAA official on the way down and that gave Duncan and me a lot of pleasure. But really I had to feel sorry for Eddie on the day. There he was, the only man breaking two hours and no-one is interested. I still have the ladies' wash-bag I was given as a prize. It's a treasured possession."

And that prize was received after having gone home and changed and then headed for the dance at the Town Hall. "It was the first time I recall meeting George MacPherson. I literally bumped into him at the door where he was standing with a collar having hurt his neck. We both had a lot of fun from the Ben Race after that."

Content with having established her record-breaking mark, Kathleen never again ran the race although both she and her own family continued to support the occasion, with her son Andrew running in it and providing assistance of all sorts. "I had done what I set out to do, and I didn't really see any point in doing it again. It was for other people to pick up the challenge and we got a lot out of it as a family over the years. I suppose in many ways I did it for Duncan. It was fun and we have all enjoyed every minute of it."

The Connochie family who contributed an enormous amount to the success of the Ben Nevis Race over the years. From left: Kathleen, Mrs Frances Connochie, Anne, Dr. C. Connochie and James. Jean Connochie, Kathleen's sister is missing from this photograph.

An appeal to local businesses for prizes to assist with the escalating costs of the race proved successful and Eddie Campbell and all the other competitors benefited accordingly.

For the record, Eddie led newcomers Pat Moy and Stan Horn up the left hand side of the Red Burn to lose them in thick mist. It was also the year that Andy Hume of Lochaber finished in third place, having cycled in to Fort William from Fersit sixteen miles away. They are made of stern stuff, the true Ben Race runners!

It was now costing some £200 to stage the race, compared with £40 just four years earlier. However with £115 having been taken at the gate and a further £15 from the sale of programmes, it was hoped that a balance would be held in hand for 1956 when all the expenses were paid.

And in another sign of the times, the team prize left Lochaber for the first time, Pat Moy (of whom much later), J. Timmins and S. Horn winning for Glasgow and District 'B'. Had Jimmy Conn, Andy Hume and Eddie Campbell been running as a team however, that would not have happened.

More threatening perhaps in the long term, was the presence of three runners from across the border - J. Hand and R. Shaw of Carlisle and J. J. Hewitt of Cambridge. Running as "England" they came second in the team competition.

1955 was to be the last time the runners ran the first 50 yards out through the main gate. Jimmy Conn reckoned he paid the penalty for over-training having been up the Ben no less than 26 times with Eddie in training.

Kathleen Connochie's dramatic contribution to the 1955 Ben Race may in fact have been the single most important factor in the explosion of interest which was to follow. The media exposure she attracted was almost certainly responsible for the fact that double the number of runners completed the course on September 1, 1956. Kathleen could not however lay any claim to the men's record. That was superbly dealt with by 23-year old Pat Moy of Vale of Leven who completed the course in one hour forty-five minutes and fifty-five seconds, taking one minute and nine seconds off Brian Kearney's best time of 1954.

There were in fact three records broken that day - the race time, the number of entrants and the number of spectators - some 2,000 for the first time. Even the weather was better with conditions described as perfect. It was warm and sunny with unlimited visibility as the 54 runners, led by Inverness Girls Pipe Band assembled at the new plaque erected on the wall of the King George V Park before setting off on the crack of the pistol fired by Baillie J. MacPherson.

There was great amusement at the start as a local schoolboy James MacAskill of Lundavra Crescent set out to follow the runners, "which amusement," according to the Highland News , "changed to pride when it was learned that he had reached the summit in about one hour and fifty minutes, tired but happy. A gallant effort of a future Ben runner!" (He did in fact run the race in the sixties) .

Pat Moy was first to the summit in one hour and twelve minutes with Stan Horn of Garscube Harriers, an international marathon runner, and Lochaber's own Eddie Campbell and Brian Kearney close behind.

The Kearney boots - On the way down Brian burst his boot when leading through rough scree. One apocryphal version of what happened next suggests that he removed a shoe from a dozing spectator, but the truth is more that he struggled gamely on in bare feet until he accepted replacements (tackety boots in fact) from the late Sauchie MacKay of Inverlochy lower down. The incident was to cost him the race however but he still managed to finish fourth. He also had to give the boots back to Sauchie junior, whose father was stranded up the Ben barefoot. Brian meanwhile walked home barefoot.

Pat Moy held on to win in the record time and his efforts ensured that the first six all finished under the two hour mark. Indeed 44 of the runners completed in under three hours and just one failed to finish. It was the first time that the runners took the back road into the Park for the finish, running over the field for the last 100 yards or so.

1956 - (left to right) P. Moy, Vale of Leven, S. Horn, Garscube, Eddie Campbell, Fort William.

Campbell, Kearney and Conn once again took the team trophy for their third, fourth and seventh finish, beating off the other eleven teams by a long distance. And there were three new trophies presented for the first time by the BNRA - The Veterans' Challenge Cup for competitors over 40 which had been donated by Charles Steel; the Lochaber Shield for the first local runner home apart from the winner, donated by the Lochaber and District Co-Operative Society and the Visitors' Shield for the first visitor apart from the winner, presented by the BNRA itself. The veterans' cup went to 40-year old Stanley Bradshaw of Clayton-le-Moors who finished in 19th place; the Lochaber Shield to Eddie Campbell and the Visitors' Shield to Stan Horn. Daniel MacQueen of Shettleston Harriers came in 41st having celebrated his 52nd birthday. It was his third race.

1956 also saw the first publication of the third of three books or booklets which have been invaluable in the compilation of this present volume. Priced one shilling, Charles Steel's short history "The Ben Nevis Race" set down for the record the runners and finishers up to that point, most valuably of all perhaps, going back as far as William Swan.

And it is in the foreword to that little booklet that Donald G. Duff MBE, MC, FRCS (Edin), himself a mountaineer of some note, who was regularly to be found in the summit party on race days, accorded the Ben Race the accolade of "supreme test of athletic stamina" which has been used in the sub-title of this account of the last 100 years.

> There is little doubt that when all the factors involved are more widely realised, the "Ben Race" will be recognised as a supreme test of athletic stamina in Britain. The further development of radio and television will popularise the event and the expansion of easy communications will yearly open up this area to more visitors from the south.
>
> Ben Nevis, justifiably acclaimed as the grandest mountain mass in Britain, holds itself supreme, not only by virtue of its 4,406 feet of height, but by the diversity of its rock conformations and of its panoramic prospects. Nowhere else in these islands can one ascend from sea level to a great height so readily and nowhere else be subjected to so rapid a change of climate and barometric pressure. Snow is present on the Ben practically always throughout the year - over 140 inches have been measured on the top in May, and even at the end of June the old Observatory building has been found completely covered.
>
> The temperature at the summit is usually 16 degrees below that registering at the base - the barometer is of course 4.5° lower. Sunshine is almost half that got yearly in Fort William, and rainfall more than twice as much. One may leave the base in fine summery weather and run into an Arctic blizzard at the top.
>
> No wonder, then, that the experienced mountaineer treats "The Ben" with the greatest respect; there are too many examples before him where ignorance and carelessness have exacted the ultimate penalty.
>
> It will be seen, therefore, that this is no task for the narrowly specialised athlete. It is a test of all-round physiological fitness - mental as well as physical - under conditions unobtainable elsewhere. Training must be long and especially devoted.
>
> So it is that those who know the conditions will look on the winners in this unique contest as supreme examples of disciplined exaltation of nervous and muscular efficiency - a class of supermen - a stimulus that we need only too much in this age of subservience to machines. We hope, then, that the work of the Ben Race Association will go on from strength to strength in the spirit, if not the letter, of the Gaelic "old word" - "Anail a' Ghàidheil, air a' mhullach." (The true Gael stops for breath only at the top).

The success of the 1956 race in fact prompted a call for it to be held on a Wednesday afternoon in the Glasgow Fair as it would attract the largest number of visitors. In a letter to *The Oban Times* the week after the race, Mr K. Stewart of Grange Road also suggested that "real runners would give up a day's pay to show their prowess in one of the toughest of all mountain marathons."

His view, however, was not all that well received:

IDEA OF THE BEN NEVIS RACE

1 Drumfada Terrace,
Corpach
10 September, 1956

Sir,

May I reply to Mr. K. Stewart's letter re Ben Nevis Race, not as the secretary but as a private person.

What Mr. Stewart does not take into consideration is that the date of the first Saturday in September has been chosen for weather reasons and also because it does not clash with other very important athletic meetings in the South.

May I also point out that a Saturday does not cause a serious loss of pay to competitors, mainly because Saturday is not usually worked in the South.

Also whilst considering shop-keepers, are not the factory workers to be considered? If the total is to be taken into consideration shopkeepers and their assistants would be very much in the minority, and their needs are helped as much as possible by starting the race as late as possible.

As for Fair Week, don't forget runners may also may be on holiday, and while the proof of success for a small entry of locals to its present day importance in athletic events commenced from the date of the Saturday race.

I am, etc., H.V. Manley

(*The Oban Times*, September 15, 1956)

In the end they didn't have to give up their hard-earned wages. The Ben Race was now firmly established as a national athletic event and accounts showed an outlay of nearly £285 which included nearly £150 for prizes, cups and medals. The income was £320 which was made up of more or less equal parts: members' fees, and donations, money raised at functions and gate takings.

1957 - Brian Kearney, Jimmy Conn, Eddie Campbell.

A year later on September 7, 1957, a record 76 runners assembled on the starting line where Olympic athlete Chris Brasher set them on their way at 3.30pm on Saturday, September 7. 63 of them were eventually to complete the course but one, 27- year old John Rix of Surrey, died as he was being carried down the mountain on a stretcher. His sad death, despite the best efforts of a search party which struggled for nine hours to locate him, following his decision to wander from the path some 2,500 feet up the mountain, is the only one recorded during a race. In many ways that is a remarkable statistic given the number of runners who have accepted the challenge.

Mr Rix was found sheltering behind a boulder, suffering from severe exposure having failed to make contact with the searching party. The sad event cast a gloom over the race and inevitably took some of the gloss off Brian Kearney's third victory, in one hour forty-six minutes and four seconds, just nine seconds outside the record.

His time was again all the more remarkable given the appalling conditions in which the race was run - high winds and driving rain. Rix apart, however, there were no casualties, with a number of runners who were taken to the Belford Hospital with cuts and bruises, making a speedy recovery.

One un-named 50-year old runner summed up conditions thus in the Scots Magazine: "I collapsed near the top. I've been running for thirty years but have never experienced conditions like those on the Ben this time. It was the cold, the wind and the pelting hailstones that beat us. Eventually my mind and body were numbed, but I just ran until I dropped. It was a nightmare, slithering and stumbling down the mountainside."

The race itself had attracted plenty of interest:

BEN RACE DAY

Tug-o-war Teams To Enter. A great deal of interest has been aroused over the news that Mr. Donald Kennedy, Lochyside has entered a Fort William tug-o-war team to challenge the strong B.A. Co's team on Ben Race Day. The Cameron Highlanders have also entered and a cart horse team known as Railway Ex. is also pulling. These events will take place on the King George V Park during the Race along with 5-a-side football and basketball exhibitions as well as dancing and piping by the Inverness Ladies Pipe Band.

(The Oban Times, August 31, 1957)

1957 - the start - Brian Kearney, as ever, led from the front.

Another new trophy was presented for the first time, the Newcomers' Shield, for the first newcomer apart from the winner. Donated by Mr J. MacPherson, it was taken south by N. G. Addison. And another new name appeared in the race credits, Dave Spencer of Barrow, himself to be numbered amongst the greats in a few years' time. In 1956 he finished in third place, eight minutes behind Brian Kearney. He was soon to be showing the full field the way home himself, winning the next three races in succession. Stanley Bradshaw meanwhile won the veterans' cup for the second successive year. Daniel MacQueen of Shettleston was still running at 54 years of age, although he failed to finish, along with a few others who found the going too much.

The headlines accompanying the race reports were inevitably on the damaging side and for all that much of the responsibility for Mr Rix's predicament lay entirely with himself, (he wore only a singlet and shorts and had strayed from the path) the image of the safety-conscious race was severely dented and much of the positive hype surrounding Kathleen Connochie's run the previous year undone.

BEN NEVIS RACE TRAGEDY
DEATH OF ENGLISH COMPETITOR

On Saturday a 24-year old English runner, Mr. J. Rix, 110 Sayes Court Farm, Addlestone, Surrey, died after competing in the annual 14-mile Ben Nevis race organised by the Ben Nevis Race Association. Twelve of the 76 entrants were unable to finish the course and three were taken to Belford Hospital, Fort William, suffering from exhaustion and exposure. One of them, it is believed, is likely to be detained for some time.

A search party found Mr. Rix about 1,000 feet from the summit early on Sunday morning. He was unconscious when found and died while being carried down the mountain. The first indication that anything had happened to him came when an official reported that he had not checked in at the summit, and when he did not report after the finish of the race a search party, consisting of police, local mountaineers, and an R.A.F. mountain rescue team, set off from Fort William in a rainstorm about 11 p.m. They found Mr. Rix near the Red Burn quite close to the track marked out for the competitors. He was in a hollow under a rock and had no shoes on, and there were cuts and bruises on his arms and legs. It was his first attempt at a Ben Nevis race.

There was heavy rain and a gale when the race started from the King George V field at Fort William. Conditions were so bad that the sports normally held in conjunction with the race were cancelled. Mr. Rix was a member of New Hall and Woodham Athletic Club.

The race was won by Brian Kearney, a Fort William brick-layer, who is twenty-eight years of age. His time was 1 hr. 46 min. 4 sec. - nine seconds over the time taken by Pat Moy, Vale of Leven Harriers, last year's winner.

(*Inverness Courier*, Tuesday, September 10, 1957)

There is little doubt but that lessons were learned on that fatal day. While there is general acknowledgement that nothing more could have been done to save the unfortunate John Rix, precautions were taken to ensure that another fatality could not happen if at all avoidable.

Although the committee have still to discuss the future of the race in the light of Saturday's tragedy, individual members feel it would be a mistake to cancel it for the future. Mr. H. Fraser, the vice chairman, said that while the circumstances of Rix's death were regrettable and unfortunate, he personally did not think it would be justified in abandoning the race.

Another Committee member said: "I still feel the race should continue to be held as it offers quite a challenge of fitness and endurance to the youth of our nation."

Later, Rix's wife, Memory Jean Rix arrived in Fort William and told race officials that her husband had been unfit to run in the race. She agreed to a post mortem which was held at the Belford Hospital. Afterwards the Race Committee held a special meeting at which the doctor's opinion on why Rix died was given.

Rix is being buried in Coventry today(Thursday). His parents are in Rhodesia and his father is flying home for the funeral.

WONDERFUL RACE FOR THE WINNER: When the runners set out the rain was lashing down, driven by high winds and the mountain was invisible in the murk. The winner was Brian Kearney who, despite the conditions - and it must be remembered that the summit of Ben Nevis is equivalent to 1,000 miles north - ran a wonderful nine seconds outside the record. He arrived in as fresh as paint - so fresh indeed that he vaulted the Barrier to meet his brother who had his outdoor kit waiting. Chaired and cheered by a host of friends and a surging audience of wide-eyed youngsters, it was a great victory over the elements and an outstanding performance. His time was 1 hr 46 mins 4 seconds. Second was N.G. Addison from Killin whose time was 1.54.13; D.A. Spencer, Barrow-in Furness, came third in 1.54.37 and Eddie Campbell was 4th in 1.55.30.

While many coming to the tape looked fresh, others looked all in but not so the hardy runner who had a swim in the Nevis river after the race, nor again the local runner who had to contend with a small terrier biting his leg as he came in over the last mile. None of the runners protested over the conditions and the 800 crowd in the park seemed oblivious to the sodden conditions and rain as they cheered on the hardy boys. Mr. Chris Brasher, who was the starter, was at the tape to welcome the runners home. The radio link was provided by the 540 LAA Regt. RATA (the Lovat Scouts under Lt. Col. M. Reeves.

Pat Moy, the record holder, did not run as he had pulled a muscle. The prize-giving was held between showers on the Parade in the evening with Chris Brasher presenting them. He said that Brian Kearney's performance was one of the most incredible he had ever seen. In fact he certainly could not have done what Kearney had in the atrocious conditions. Provost Mrs. Murphy proposed the votes of thanks and congratulated the runners for putting Fort William on the map. The Inverness Ladies Pipe Band then beat Retreat.

(*The Oban Times*, September 14, 1957)

BEN NEVIS RACE ASSOCIATION

This Certificate is presented to:

B. KEARNEY.

of FORT WILLIAM.

and certifies that he took part in the

BEN NEVIS RACE

OF 19 57

and completed the course in One hours 46 minutes 4 seconds

Date 7th September 1957.

Hon. Secretary.

BEN NEVIS RACE ASSOCIATION

1957 was the last time Brian Kearney graced the Ben Race and his performance that day was indeed a magnificent achievement. "Probably my best ever," he says himself. At 27 and in his prime, Brian Kearney decided to quit at the top, devoting himself to other pursuits such as his beloved sailing.

And fame came easily. When attending in the Palace Hotel on the evening of the Race a star-struck individual from Lochaber approached the master, who was discussing the race with Chris Brasher. Modestly, Brian stepped aside, allowing the local worthy to approach the Olympian. To everyone's amusement however, it was the Kearney autograph which was required!

A Whist Drive held in Fort William shortly after raised some funds which were contributed to a special fund set up by the Ben Nevis Race Association to aid the dependants of John Rix. The 1958 Race programme spelled out the message learned by everyone involved in 1957.

> Everything possible is done both to provide for the welfare of the competitors in the interests of security. The arrangements of the Association, based on years of experience, are well nigh perfect. They brief the Lovat Scouts for their work of radio-communication. The various units, each complete with a radio set, are stationed at the summit, at the half-way point, at the foot (Achintee) in direct communication with the main control on King George V Field. On the outward journey as the runners pass Achintee, signals are passed to King George V Field and broadcast from there. Furthermore, so that no runner can lose himself in mist, each station clears them all in turn, and the summit unit does not leave its post until every runner has passed down on his return journey. Other voluntary officials do duty as markers at particular points on the mountain, as time-keepers on the summit and on the field, and as medical and welfare officers.

One step taken to avoid the possibility of late finishers being caught on the hill was to bring the start forward an hour, to 2.30pm. All competitors were insured against accidents during the race covering a weekly amount of £6 per week for six weeks, providing a medical certificate was obtained.

Only six failed to finish and it did not appear to be long before the 100 barrier would be broken. And Daniel MacQueen was still there, now aged 54, finishing remarkably in just under three hours (02.59.28).

1957 - THE FINISH.
It was David Spencer's first win and he promised to be back the following year. It was the first time
the MacFarlane Cup had crossed the border. It wasn't to be the last. The best visitor apart from the
winner was Frank Dawson of Salford in second place - another Englishman and Jimmy Conn won
the "Best Local" Shield for the first time after seven races.

The race was run in a thunderstorm and with 1957 still fresh in everyone's minds,
there was some discussion as to whether the event should in fact be postponed.
However it wasn't, and there was no stopping Dave Spencer who raced away with
victory, coming home in one hour forty-six minutes and eight seconds, thirteen
seconds outside Pat Moy's record.

1958
The starter was Mr Malcolm McCulloch CBE, DL, Chief Constable, City of Glasgow Police. He set 82 runners on their way, an increase of 14 on the previous year, indicating that safety was not a worry for the runners.   *Jimmy Murdoch*

A.A Robertson of Reading AC in fourteenth place won the veterans' award for the first time, finishing in two hours four minutes and seventeen seconds. Lochaber AC 'A' in their first competitive appearance on the Ben (Conn, Campbell and D. L Thomson) won the team trophy. Brian Kearney was, by the way, one of four hill markers for the 1958 race.

Tartan kilts and wellie boots were the order of the day at the Marquee Dance later in the evening and Vauxhall Motors (eleventh in the team race) were left to wonder what to do with the cars they took up for the race. As Eddie Campbell pointed out: "How were they to know there was no road up Ben Nevis?"

> **In a remarkably short time they hove in sight, their multi-coloured slips a serpent of colour along the path. I saw bald heads and I saw fresh boyish faces and once a fine fuzz of black beard. The rain held its fire to this point, but suddenly as the panting mob breasted the first steep slopes it let go, with a flash of lightning and a crack of thunder which sent us under a boulder for shelter, but we were soaked to the skin just the same.**

Forty minutes later the first runner appeared on the return journey. It was not the winner, but that great veteran Dunky Wright, now over 60 and a former British Empire Games marathon champion, had entered for a bit of fun, but now he was gently making his own way back, having given the weather and the treacherous path best. Only twenty minutes afterwards the first man from the summit came bounding downhill, wonderfully sure-footed on the slippery mud and stones, and undoubtedly this man, David Spencer, of Barrow, would have broken the existing record had underfoot conditions been more reasonable. At 1 hour 46 minutes 8 seconds for the 13 mile course he was only 13 seconds behind the record closely followed by another Englishman, Frank Dawson, of Salford, with the Scottish record-holder, Pat Moy, of Vale of Leven, third.

Watching some of the others come stumbling downhill, slithering out of control and taking some heavy falls, I felt sure that the majority of runners had chosen the wrong footgear, and should have had something spiky to give a grip instead of the ordinary plimsolls, which act like a ski on a wet mountainside. The winner wore rubber studs in his shoes, and future competitors would be advised to do the same.

Every runner who took part in this race to 4406 feet in such a wild storm is worthy of admiration, and none more so than the lad who came in last, namely Derek Leviston, of Barrow, aged 19, who was running only the second race of his life and probably the toughest he is ever likely to experience. Few saw him come in after his three-hour ordeal, his arm bloody from a fall on the way down and his reserves of energy nearly at their end, but he had the grit to finish. A fine performance.

(Tom Weir, *Scots Magazine*, November, 1958)

The 3,000 spectators who turned up to watch the 1959 race set a new record themselves. Race starter Chief Constable McCulloch set off a record 94 runners (out of 130 who had been listed in the programme) at 2.30pm. One who arrived late, having travelled from south of the border, rushed up to the start, divesting himself of his outer garments!

And it was 22-year old Dave Spencer, wearing 100, who was to lead 87 other runners home, including the remarkable Daniel MacQueen (now 55) who came in 84th in three hours thirteen minutes and twenty-nine seconds. Eddie Campbell's and C. P. Wilson's record of two successive wins had been matched. Only three runners failed to complete the course and the prizes were presented by another sporting legend, Olympic boxer Dick MacTaggart.

Spencer's time of one hour forty-seven minutes and fifty-three seconds was enough to take him home nearly four minutes ahead of J. Lineker of Pitreavie and Frank Dawson who had to settle for third place this time.

Jimmy Conn was again the best local finisher, in fifth place, compared to his fourth of the previous year. Pitreavie "A" were the top team out of nine, six of which were a strong English contingent. Kathleen Connochie meanwhile had now established herself on the BNRA committee, having spurned all attempts to persuade her to run again.

Eddie Campbell with Dave Spencer, winner in 1959 (and 58 and 60!)

The North of Scotland Milk Marketing Board awarded a new prize in 1959 to the youngest competitor under three hours and thirty minutes - a colour camera. The first winner was J. Slocket from Clayton-le-Moors who came in 82nd.

People's Journal

INVERNESS AND NORTHERN
COUNTIES

No. 5272.   JANUARY 24, 1959.   Price 3d.

Out of this croft come champions

JUST over a year ago the Lochaber Athletic Club (better known in the Fort William area as the L.A.C.) got the lease of a 100-year-old croft for a club hut.

It was a tumbledown place with crumbling walls, and the first meeting was held by the light of a paraffin lamp.

The L.A.C. was the dream of **Messrs Charles Steel** and **Alistair Macmillan**, both of whom agreed that Lochaber would never produce a worthwhile athletic team unless all those interested got together.

With a strong committee headed by **Mr Duncan McIntyre**, a well-known Ben Nevis runner, as president, d a n c e s were arranged to provide funds.

But the club could not afford tradesmen to carry out renovations, so they decided to do the job themselves.

A grant was obtained, and plans for a committee room, showers and a bath were drawn up.

A new floor was laid by **Brian Kearney** (" the king of the mountains ").

The ceiling was boarded up under the direction of joiner **Ewan McDonald**, who motorcycles over 12 miles to train.

Plumbing and plastering were carried out by **Jimmy Conn** and **Hughie Cameron.**

Electric light was installed.

The work of providing showers and baths is to be started shortly. And the boys still find time to win races.

Plumber and captain Jimmy Conn was second in the Cairngorm race and third in the N.S. cross-country championships.

● *Three peaks' record*

The 1958 winner of the latter event is **Eddie Campbell**, who was second in the Goatfell and third in the Cairngorm races.

He and **Andy Hume** are the only runners in Lochaber to hold the Scottish marathon standard medal.

Brian Kearney has won the Ben Nevis, Cairngorm and Goatfell races and holds the record for the three peaks.

The L.A.C. has also won the team race in the Ben Nevis race and the North of Scotland cross-country championships.

The fair sex is represented in the club, too — 18 - year - old **Wilma Rutherford** is a sprint and long jump specialist. At the 1958 Inverness gathering she was first in the ladies' long jump and second in both the North of Scotland A.A.A. 100 yards and the open 220 yards.

Two individuals, Charles Steel and Alister MacMillan, were largely responsible for the formation of Lochaber AC in 1958. A 100-year old croft was leased for a club hut and a committee formed. Eventually, with the help of tradesmen who were runners, a new club-house was built and the club went from strength to strength.

The trophies were all, incidentally, for the first time inscribed with the winners' names before the presentation in a tradition which has been maintained.

With safety paramount, one competitor who suffered an attack of stomach pains at the summit, found himself being treated by D.G. Duff (FRCS) who was with the summit party. All in all, with near perfect weather conditions contributing to fourteen times under two hours, the memories of 1957 were safely set aside, but not forgotten. The race's reputation had been completely restored as a premier athletic event.

By now Lochaber's reputation as a club was well known as well. Eddie Campbell had won the 1958 North of Scotland Cross-country championships with Jimmy Conn third. Eddie was also second in the Goatfell race and third in the Cairngorm race. He and Andy Hume of Fersit were the only runners in Lochaber to hold the Scottish marathon standard medal at the time. Brian Kearney had by now won Goatfell, the Ben and the Cairngorm races and held the records for all three.

1959 start   *Jimmy Dunlevy*

Dave Spencer - a Ben Race Great.   *Jimmy Dunlevy*

And if ever its sporting credibility was enhanced it was in 1960. The race was attracting solo and club entrants from all over the country and 144 were listed to start under the instruction of Mr Hobbs of Inverlochy Castle.

All the big names were there apart, perhaps, from Brian Kearney and the apparently indestructible Daniel MacQueen. Now 56 (although Eddie Campbell appears to have found him two extra years in his booklet) the unfortunate Daniel was barred from running in the 1960 race because he had taken part in the Billy Butlin walk from John o'Groats to Land's End, a professional event. Bureaucracy had once again dealt the race an unwieldy blow. But Daniel ran the race all the same, setting off in his own time.

Fifteen teams had entered the race and the best returns yet saw 97 finishers, the biggest field to date, with the first dozen under two hours. The weather no doubt helped - dry at the start, wet and misty at half way, a cold wind on the summit. More or less classic Ben Race weather. And Lochaber regained the team trophy.

But the most remarkable aspect of the race was its finish. With M. Vickers of Barrow leading the field, he realised his win would prevent Dave Spencer his club-mate from winning a unique third successive race. In what must rank as the most selfless gesture of the Ben Race of all time, Vickers stood aside and allowed Spencer to win his coveted hat-trick.

Spencer was later allegedly seen loading his car with oatmeal, and gallons of water from Ben Nevis's famous "whisky burn" and when asked what he was up to, replied that he was going to try an experiment on his team-mates back home!

J.W. Hobbs, Inverlochy Castle, started the race at 2.40p.m. from the King George V Park. The visibility at the top was clear but poor halfway up. It was hoped that the fine drizzle and the lack of sunshine might ensure a new record but this was not to be.

David Spencer, Barrow AC, was the winner for the third consecutive year in a time of 1.52.22. - 2nd was M. Vickers, Barrow AC, 1.52.23 with many thinking it was in fact a deadheat. It seemed that Vickers, the fresher of the two runners, could easily have overtaken his club-mate, but he sportingly gave his friend every encouragement and rejoiced that his club mate had achieved a hat-trick of victories.

The first six came very close to each other; 3rd was J. Conn, Lochaber AC, Eddie Campbell was 6th.

Present at the race were Sir Malcolm MacCulloch, former chief constable of Glasgow, Chief Constable Johnstone, Inverness, Provost & Mrs. Duncan Grant and Sheriff Reid Kerr.

A feature of this year's race was a charities fair run by Fort William Round Table. The crowd was 2,000.

NO CASUALTIES: everybody completed the race, including D. MacQueen who came in second last in 3.38.00.

Torrential downpour scattered the prizewinner and the attendant crowd as J.W. Hobbs handed over the awards. The youngest competitor was Brian Hatch (17) of Lochaber AC. The fastest veteran was S. Bradshaw, Clayton-le-Moors. At a dance in the Town Hall Miss Jean Mac Lean, Roy Bridge, was chosen as Miss Ben Nevis.

(*The Oban Times*, September 10, 1960)

T.P O'Reilly (Springburn Harriers) leading a pack of runners across Nevis Bridge, including No 55, the eventual winner Dave Spencer and No 93 M. Vickers, who enabled him to secure his remarkable win.

And talking of sportsmanship, in 1960, Jimmy Conn completed a remarkable sequence of 9 races coming home in third place this time. It was his third successive best local performance. The win he coveted so much was to elude him forever though and he must go down as the finest runner (certainly from Lochaber) who never won the ultimate accolade.

As to Eddie Campbell, he completed his tenth race (all under two hours) in sixth place, the only person to complete the full set in the 1950s. He was still there in 1994 having run every year apart from the fateful 1980 race which was cancelled due to bad weather.

While Eddie ran them all, (seen here finishing in 1994 - the only "Sunshine" on the day was the one clapping!), several ran once and never again, and not just Kathleen Connochie.

Several other outstanding achievements were recorded in 1960. B. Smith came all the way from Hamilton Olympia in Canada to finish in twelfth place and the best newcomer J. Severen of Tipton finished fourth, edging out the excellent Frank Dawson who completed a fine sequence of results in fifth place, one ahead of Eddie Campbell. Stanley Bradshaw the redoubtable veteran completed his second "double" and was amongst the prize-winners greeted at the Parade at 8pm by Mr J.W Hobbs of Inverlochy Castle.

All that is best about the Ben Race was there for all to see in 1960. Great athletes and great sportsmanship and the end of a golden era.

The spirit of the Ben Race was perhaps never better epitomised than in the kenspeckle figure of Jock Petrie, and the youthful exuberance of Kathleen Connochie. A great sportsman in a Great Era.

Kathleen Connochie with Duncan MacIntyre

The Herald

A. Gillespie

"It is really two huge mountains rolled into one, with a lake or tarn nestling between the two shoulders. Vegetation exists up to the height of about 3,000 feet, but beyond that, only occasional clumps of verdure are met with."

W. T. Kilgour, *Twenty Years on Ben Nevis*

Chapter 6

1961-1970
More Greats, new records

David Spencer's first win in 1959 marked the beginning of a spell of domination of the race by English runners, right through until 1965. Allan MacRae of Lairg in 1966 and Robert Shields of Clydebank a year later, broke that run.

And if the Golden Era of the 1950s was dominated by Eddie Campbell and Brian Kearney, the name of Michael P. Davies, a London school teacher and life-long friend of Eddie's following his exploits, is writ large in the history books. Davies is, along with Campbell, arguably the race's greatest ever runner, and certainly the most consistent with three wins and second place five times.

And the times being recorded for the race ("the strenuous effort" as it was described in the 1962 programme) were nearly all remarkable in fact with just eight minutes covering the winners in the race from 1953 to 1962 when 20-year old Peter Hall from Barrow set a new mark of one hour forty-five minutes and forty-four seconds, eleven seconds better than the time set by Pat Moy of Vale of Leven in 1956. Hall was eventually to write himself into the history books with four consecutive wins from 1962. His feat remains unmatched to this day.

MacRae's croft was home to many Lochaber athletes in the late fifties and early sixties.

Left to right: Pat Neish, Hamish Loudon, Billy Hatch, Jo Campbell, Jimmy Conn, Eddie Campbell, Donald MacDonald, with Nigel Chisholm to the fore.

137

Fort William & Lochaber News:

NEVIS RACE RECORD

Major Honours Go over The Border

There was a crowd of 2,500 at the Town Park to see 149 runners start in dry conditions at sea level which gave way to mist on the mountain. Peter Hall, Barrow AC., set a new record of 1.45.44 - 11 seconds better than that of Pat Moy, Vale Of Leven in 1956. As Hall crossed the finishing line at walking pace, he did not think that he had broken the record. 2nd: M.P. Davies, (Reading AC) was one minute behind; he was last year's winner; 3rd Harry Clayton, Bristol AC in 1.47.54.

Eddie Campbell led the Lochaber contingent of Michael Moan, William Hatch, Nigel A. Chisholm, Douglas Thomson, James A. MacAskill, Jimmy Conn, Alasdair Morrison, Hugh Cameron, Andrew Hume and Malcolm Cameron. Eddie finished 23rd in 1.58.44. Nigel Chisholm was 29th and Jimmy Conn came in 33rd. 21 Teams competed.

The race was started by Mr. Donald G. Duff, formerly of the Belford Hospital. A tent manned by Baillie Mrs. Murphy and her husband who were showing the famous athlete, Cameron of Muccomir's belt. This attracted a great deal of attention and raised funds for the West Highland Museum.

(*The Oban Times*, September 8, 1962)

Ben Nevis Race Prospects
GURKHAS IN PEAK FORM FOR BIG TEST

Great interest is being shown in the entry of 12 officers from the 1/6 O.E.D Gurkha Rifles. They have been in training on the mountain for the past four weeks. Heightened by the fact that Rifleman Lalbahadur Pun won the hill race at the Glenurquhart Highland Games in 21mins 36seconds.

In all, 227 runners have entered and there is a waiting list. A goodwill message has been received from the planning officer in Anchorage, Alaska who states that he regards the Ben Nevis Race as the greatest mountain race in the world.

(*The Oban Times*, September 5, 1963)

BEN RECORD BROKEN

192 Starters including the Gurkha team. There was the biggest ever crowd of spectators making the whole day a memorable one as the record was again reduced. It was a wet day with the mist well down the mountain. Starter was Lt. Col. D.J.S. Murray, C.O. 4/5 Queen's Own Cameron Highlanders.

Returning runners looked fresh although a number were cut about the legs. 2 lost their shoes and completed the course barefoot. The Gurkhas were slow up the hill but came down at a cracking pace.

The winner was Peter Hall, first last year, who broke his own record of 1.45.44 by finishing in 1.41.45. 2nd Michael Davies (also second last year) also broke the old record, finishing in 1.42.45. 3rd: Gurkha Rifleman Lalbahadur Pun who also broke the old record. He finished in 1.45.36.

The team trophy went to the Parachute Regiment; 2nd: Barrow AC; 183 finished. The Colonel presented the trophies in a marquee in the evening.

800 dancers finished off a great day to the music of the Blue Stars and Rebels in a marquee.

(*The Oban Times*, September 12, 1963)

Donald MacDonald, Lochaber AC, 1963

Cableway for Ben Nevis

After a site meeting it was agreed to form a development company to raise funds to build a cableway up the Ben. The meeting was attended by local landowners and a helicopter expert along with the county planning officer and brought forward a scheme which has been under consideration for many years.

Behind the scheme: Cameron of Locheil, the Scottish Tourist Board assisted by Allan Bateman, a Fort William businessman, and Mr. J. Hamilton, a Glasgow chartered mechanical engineer. Experts believed that the cable way could be put up in two stages and would take 18 months to complete.

A survey was carried out in 1935 and the estimated cost then was £25,000, but it would take ten times that now.

"We are expected to gain widespread support for the cableway," said Mr. Bateman, "we have the precedent of the Cairngorm chair lift."

The Provost, Rev. G.K.B. Henderson thought the cableway would be an ideal tourist attraction but he advised that the road up the Ben would have to be improved before such a scheme could be undertaken.

(*The Oban Times*, August 20, 1964)

There was huge interest in the 1964 race, with Peter Hall's attempt to win the race for a third successive time the main focus of attention. There were 186 entries, 20 down on last year, with a 30-strong army contingent. Many more would have been present but for overseas' commitments.

And they came from far and wide to take up the challenge - first time competitor George Coleman, an Olympic walker and a Hungarian. Eddie Campbell was reported to be in good form having won the hill race at the Glenurquhart Games the week before. A new rescue bag, designed by Dr. J. S. Berkeley and manufactured by a Greenock firm, was to be used in cases of exposure.

New Ben Race Record

Peter Hall, Barrow AC, made it 3 in a row and broke his own record again. Despite adverse conditions of high winds and rain he returned a time of 1.38.50 just under 3 minutes better than last year.

He led throughout and reached the summit in just under an hour. There was a crowd of around 1,000 who were undeterred by the elements. He came into their view in 1.35.00, coming through the show ground at MacRae's croft and was applauded all the way to the finish.

143 started. Mountain conditions were poor, visibility on the top was down to 10 yards and got worse throughout the race.

Hall, looking very fresh, said that conditions were better than last year, although the rain slowed him down. He hoped to be back next year and thought it was possible to reduce the time under 1.30.00. In recognition of his record he received a replica of the MacFarlane Cup.

Michael Davies (Reading AC), winner in 1961 and 2nd last year, was again runner-up. 3rd was R. Lewney, Barrow AC.

1st Scot was Ronald Coleman, Dundee Hawkhill Harriers, in 6th place after lying 2nd for most of the ascent. Ronald, one of three Colemans in the race, has run as an Olympic possible. Alastair Wood, a well known marathon runner, was the next Scot. The biggest cheer was for Eddie Campbell, a local taxi driver, complete with beard. He came in twelfth in 1.52.35.

Fastest newcomer was David Hodgson (Leeds St. Mark's Harriers) who was 4th. Barrow won the team prize. 138 finished; there were 23 finishers under 2 hours.

Only 5 retirals and no requirement for new casualty bag.

(*The Oban Times*, September 10, 1964)

The next race attracted another international field with runners from New Zealand and Alaska amongst the 194 entrants, an increase of 12 on the previous year. With Peter Hall attempting to win his fourth successive race, there was huge interest. Some, however, would not be present to see him take up the challenge. At a committee meeting of the Race Association tribute was paid by Mr. Lachlan MacKinnon to 3 members who had died: Joseph A. MacPherson a former chairman, Victor Manley, a former secretary, and Ted Rose. *"These members are a grievous loss not only to the Ben Race Committee but to the district as a whole."*

Former runner Hugh "Bottles" Cameron, discussing the race with Allan MacRae, winner in 1966.

And at the end of the day, in front of 1,700 spectators, Peter Hall did not disappoint. He won for the fourth successive year in one hour forty-two minutes and nineteen seconds, just 38 seconds ahead of Michael Davies. David Spencer, another former winner, was third making up a truly great trio, arguably the best one-two-three ever to complete the race.

Hall led from the beginning, being 200 yards ahead by half way, and reached the summit in 01.09.00. Davies caught up on the descent and by Achintee there was little in it but Hall held on to win by 38 seconds.

He said afterwards "I did not run as well as I had expected to do. It was a fairly easy run up although there was mist blowing in my face." He was surprised that Davies had caught up with him and that spurred him on to greater efforts.

The first Scot was Ian Donald (Clydesdale Harriers) in 4th place; Eddie Campbell was 23rd. Some very young Lochaber runners showed promise for the future: John Kinghorn was 25th in 02.01.22; Sandy Reece was 43rd in 02.07.32. Michael Moan 02.14.06; John MacConnell 02.44.11; D. Thomson 03.09.34

Unattached runner Allan MacRae of Lochinver served notice of his potential and great things to come when he arrived in 6th place. Scott D. Hamilton, the planning assistant from Alaska came in 39th and delighted the crowd by doing a somersault on the finishing line. Norman Harris of the Owairaka Club New Zealand, was 42nd.

Barrow AC won the team trophy and there were only 7 retirals out of 158 starters. 27 finished in under 2 hours and 108 in under three.

No local runner had won the Ben Race since 1957. Lochaber badly needed a local win and Allan MacRae was the man who delivered it in 1967. A shepherd from Little Assynt, Lochinver near Lairg, MacRae completed the race, which was run in blistering heat with visibility on the mountain down to 100 feet at half-way and 50 at the summit, in 01.45.49. He had came to Lochaber three weeks before the race to join the locals in their preparation.

Allan MacRae, who scaled further heights in 1992 when he led the Assynt crofters' bid to buy the Assynt estate.

Allan MacRae's victory for Lochaber in 1966 was followed by another Scottish win when Robert Shields of Clydesdale Harriers, second to Allan in 1966, came home first of 131 challengers the following year.

The 1967 start, the runners were set off by Ex-Provost William "Bobo" MacKay of Inverness.

Despite conditions described as "seldom worse", fast times were recorded. Driving rain and gale force wind tested the runners to the utmost, loose stones gave no foothold and visibility between the Red Burn halfway point and the summit was practically nil.

Robert, who trained in the hills of Old Kilpatrick, came home in 01.41.11, just two minutes and two seconds outside the record.

Robert Shields, winner, 1967.

Michael Davies was second once again with Eddie Campbell the first local in tenth pace in 01.58.39. Donald Fraser was the next local, in 20th place, in 02.04.32 and Marshall Brown was 3rd local, 41st, in 02.15.15.

As late arrivals came back, soaked through, covered in mud and often bleeding, the first aid tent was said to look "like a battlefield". Four runners had to be taken to hospital, and one of them R. Bott, Maryhill Harriers, was detained overnight.

The weather was kinder, however, in 1968 - "seldom better" and the great Michael Davies took full advantage. It was the first time in 8 years, he said afterwards, he had completed a race with no mist and he was able to see his fellow competitors all the way up the mountain.

Davies' time was 01.39.39, just over half a minute outside the record. Robert Lewney of Barrow AC, third the previous year, was second in 01.45.17 with Gerald R. Stevens of Reading AC, third in 01.45.37.

There was a tremendous cheer for Donald Fraser from Caol as he crossed the line in 6th place in 01.48.40 as 1st local. The highly promising Fraser ended up with 4 awards - a bronze medal for 6th place, Co-op Shield for best local apart from the winner, Kathleen Connochie Cup for best performer under-21 apart from the winner and the Victor Manley Shield for the best local under 21.

Another local success was John Marstrand of Lochaber AC who was 16th in 1.53.27 and was awarded the C.W.S. Steel Cup for the best performance by a veteran (over 40).

The race was, however, a huge disappointment for two local runners Gerald Young of Morar and Somerled (Ronnie) MacIntosh of Spean Bridge, who were stopped by officials as they passed through the checkpoint and banned from taking part because it was alleged that they had taken part in Highland Games competitions. Their reinstatement forms were not apparently in order.

The 1967 race was one of the toughest of the decade with driving rain and gale-force winds. Robert Shields' finishing time of one hour forty-one minutes was just two minutes outside the record and a remarkable achievement.

The poor weather of 1967 was followed by a period of favourable conditions with 1968 passing as "excellent"; 1969 "quite good"; 1970 "high winds and brilliant sunshine"; and "ideal' (something of a rarity surely) in 1971.

All four were won by Englishmen, Mike Davies winning the first two, Jeff Norman of Altrincham the third and David Cannon of Kendal the fourth. Much more was to be heard of him as he went on to win no less than five times in the next six years.

And in 1968 the BNRA were once again having to cope with some bureaucratic edicts from the SAAA's. Their new Rule 4 (1) forbade the running of the race to those aged under 20. Therefore 21 entries had to be refused. There was still, however, a maximum entry of 200.

TO BEAT THE BEN

The Scots, being sensible folk, are not given to running up and down mountains for the fun of it. Maybe of course it has nothing to do with sense at all. Maybe it's just that there are too many mountains in Scotland and the Scots, never renowned for doing things by half, would prefer to run up and down all of them, or none of them. And so they prefer the latter.

There is one exception though. Today's Ben Nevis Race, which has been going strong since before the turn of the century and whose popularity indicates it will last well into the twenty hundreds.

And this once more shows the strange bent in the Scotsman's make-up — he feels that if he is going to run up and down a mountain, he might as well chose the biggest one available, all 4406 feet of it towering above the cold salt waters of Loch Linnhe.

But Ben Nevis is a challenge to more than just the Scots, and so each year we welcome athletes from the rest of Britain and from overseas. For them, as for the Scots, sensible rules like not running up and down mountains are forgotten in the face of its grandeur.

Since it resumed as an annual event in 1951, four men have dominated the race. Two of them, Brian Kearney and Eddie Campbell are from Fort William itself, and the other two, David Spencer and Peter Hall, come from Barrow in Westmoreland. Hall, indeed, is the course record holder with a time of one hour 38 minutes 50 seconds set in 1964.

The successes these men have enjoyed reveal a part of the character of this race. The two locals lived almost within touching distance of the mists on the mountain; they knew the quirks of a course which is at the mercy of the elements and which can change from a Jekyll to a Hyde from minute to minute.

The Barrow runners, on the other hand, come from a land where hill racing is a traditional part of the scene. For them the challenge of the Ben was the challenge of the Fells writ larger and more awesome. They came to the race toughened in a tough school and they conquered.

But the two most recent victors, Allan MacRae, the Lairg shepherd, and last year's winner Robert Shields, have shown such advantages as can be gained from local knowledge or from a wide experience of hill racing can be overcome. They have shown, indeed, that Ben Nevis is a great leveller and that nothing can beat sheer physical and mental will-to-win.

In the last analysis it all comes back to the mountain. It is the mountain which each year attracts 150 and more athletes to a sports event in the traditional sense of the word, where it is not the winning that counts but the taking part.

Each year, from Highlands and Lowlands, from over the Border and over the sea they come to pit their skills, not against each other, but against the mountain. Special honour goes to the man who finishes first, but honour and acclaim go to all who finish, for they have beaten Ben Nevis.

                                        (Jack Regan, 1968 Race Programme)

There were two new trophies for competition as well - the Lochiel Cup donated by Cameron of Lochiel for the best Services' team apart from the winners and the Reading Athletic Shield, donated by Reading AC for the best team affiliated to the Southern Counties Cross Country Association, apart from the winners.

By way of encouragement to the runners, the BNRA had on display courtesy of Mr George F. Simpson (then of Longniddry, East Lothian) the Austin Seven in which he ascended the Ben on October 6, 1928. The car, a standard model, reached the summit in 7 hours and 23 minutes, and returned to Achintee in just under two hours, with only a slightly bent rear mudguard to show for its ordeal. Mr Simpson was the first driver to take a vehicle to the summit and back in one day. On the next day the Austin Seven was driven back to Edinburgh without any adjustments.

As the decade drew to a close, there was no stopping Mr Consistency - Michael P. Davies, winning in 1969 for the second successive year, this time in one hour, forty-three minutes and twenty-five seconds. He was followed home by P. Watson, Bramley Harriers in 01.44.09 with W.R. Timlin (Newcastle University) 3rd in 01.44.26.

The race was started by Rt. Rev. Dr. T. M. Murchison, Moderator of the General Assembly of the Church of Scotland who joined the list of "personalities" sending the runners on their way. Seventeen of the 145 competitors who finished the course were veterans. Allan MacRae was the first local, 4th overall, in a time of 01.45.43. D.A. Fraser, Caol, was 11th and Eddie Campbell was 35th.

English runners dominated the 1970 race, which took place in high winds and brilliant sunshine, taking the first three places. 154 runners started on Duncan MacIntyre's command and 152 finished. The winner was Jeffrey Norman, an Olympic athlete and hospital pharmacist of Altrincham & Dist. AC. in 01.40.45, the third fastest time ever recorded. Dave Cannon, Kendal AC was second in 01.41.13 with Michael Davies, Reading AC third in 01.43.57. Donald A. Fraser, Caol, was again first local - 18th in 01.52.20. Eddie Campbell was 34th in 01.59.30. Still running then, and still running now.

The 1980s saw their fair share of controversy with regard to the race, but it was the decade when the rescue helicopters, seen here on an exercise, came into their own.

(A. Gillespie)

Chapter 7

1971-1991
Familiar squat cairns

The new decade saw the Ben Nevis Race move to a new home, Claggan Park, nestling at the foot of Ben Nevis itself. Fittingly, the first race at the new venue was run in ideal conditions.

The race was also notable for the fact that Eddie Campbell completed his twenty-first consecutive race inside 2 hours. Later, he was presented with a silver salver to mark the occasion. Only Peter Hall, four times winner, had won the race more often than Eddie at this point.

The new venue, Claggan Park

Over 170 started the race and it was David Cannon, Kendal AC, who led them home, establishing the new mark of 01.33.05. At that time a 21-year old linesman, he had a few months previously won the half-Ben Race. He was very closely followed by Brian Finlayson, Forth Valley Harriers, in 01.33.54.

There was another special cheer for Charlie Petrie (42, right) formerly of Caol who had returned from Canada on holiday the previous week and decided to enter.

Dave Cannon, who was to dominate the race in the mid-70s

Fair weather followed the race into 1972, which was started by Dr Charles Connochie, and conditions were such that heat exhaustion caused several of the 150 starters to retire. Notwithstanding the heat, David Cannon, Kendal AC, won in 01.32.57 managing to trim 8 seconds off the time it took him the year before in much cooler conditions.

Brian Finlayson, Lochaber AC, was second in 01.34.38 having put up a brave fight all the way up and down. Finlayson took the lead at the Red Burn on the way down, but Cannon came back to take over and lead to the finish. Third was Harry Walker, Blackburn Harriers, in 01.36.34

First veteran was John Marstrand, Lochaber AC, 19th in 01.52.28. Mike Davies, Reading AC, a three times winner, with 5 second places to his credit, was 8th.

Dave Cannon's speed to the finish was more than matched by Harry Walker, who lowered the new record even further in 1973, taking three and a half minutes off the time. The following year however, Cannon gained his revenge again, winning for the third time in 01.30.17. His nearest rivals were Brian Finlayson, Lochaber AC, in 01.31.10 and Harry Walker, in 01.31.27. These three battled it out all the way up and down, putting the rest well behind them.

DOON THE BEN

It was raining in Fort William. Figures hurried along the High Street past the hotel. Inside, in his usual corner, with slumped shoulders, sat the once proud victor of a long forgotten race. The centenary hype was passing by until, later that night, it was all to change......

Part One - The Challenge

Down stairs in the Grand, with a pint in his hand,
An Englishman looked over, choking,
"What, him in the shirt - that little squirt?
You've really got to be joking."

He pushed through the crowd, and shouted out loud,
"The last of the great record men!
I'll bet you, old sonny, any amount of money,
I could beat you down the Ben.

I've won the Nevis Race, at a new record pace.
No-one can run like I do.
I've won every event, from here down to Kent,
Now I want your record too."

Staring into my drink, I started to think,
"Why couldn't I answer the clown?
If I swallowed my fear, like I swallowed my beer;
But no - I could only look down.

"Can't run, can't jive - now can't even drive."
I heard him continue to jeer......
"I'm not surprised he was breathalysed -
He can't even hold his beer.

Looks as old as the hills and rattles with pills,
With a face like an old worn-out shoe.
Imagine him on a date! If he ever found a mate,
I doubt if he'd know what to do."

A different voice spoke - a local-sounding bloke,
"Ah now, I think there was something.
For I've heard that he keeps a wee box where he sleeps,
And in it, some say, is a ring."

"A ring!" He still raged, "So your friend was engaged."
What on earth to, d'you suppose?
What sort of old cow would wear his ring now,
Unless perhaps going through her nose!"

The table and chair went up in the air,
As I leapt up and glared in his face.
"Tomorrow at ten, at the top of the Ben
I'll give you your downhill race."

Part Two - The Race

He was drawing away, at a terrible speed,
Nothing I could do would shorten his lead.
His shape became vaguer, then faded from view.
His steps became softer, then disappeared too.
On the summit plateau, the wind lost its force,
My feet soon thawed out, on their zig-zagging course.
My hands and my body started getting warm,
And on the smooth scree banks, I clicked into form.
Familiar squat cairns, would loom up like friends,
Their yellow dye markings, would show me the bends.

Part Three - The Decision

John MacInnes, the Inspector, always finishes a lecture,
With something that I was to learn:
At this time of year, huge holes will appear,
Just under the snow on Red Burn.

If a man were to slip, he could rip off his hip,
But he was now so far below,
To have any chance at all, I must risk the fall,
So I swung off the track, into the snow.

The Vision

Sound and horizon, now all seemed to go,
As I hurtled down over that thin crust of snow.
Twenty to thirty miles an hour I'd be reaching,
Trying to shut out any thoughts of a-breeching.
"Jimmy!" Like a needle a voice pierced my brain;
I slowed down and stopped, when I heard it again.
A blue-hyphen shimmering form, was waving to me.
But against the bright white-out, I just couldn't see.
The vision now faded, but I knew who she was,

And when I looked down, I soon saw the cause -
A jagged hole had opened to the Red Burn below,
And her warning saved me from death in the snow.
Back to full speed, I was soon at half-way,
And out from the clouds, to a beautiful day.
Look away down Loch Eil to the Cuillins of Skye,
But it wasn't the view that was catching my eye.......
It was the sight of the Englishman, at "Broken Bridge" -
He was walking! He was walking down the ridge.
I passed him at the deer fence, but he didn't see me,
He flaked out on the road, when he reached Achintee.

Part Five - The Finish

With each step my hate had begun to abate
Even with Fort William in view.
Inside I'd a glow, and just seemed to know,
She'd have forgiven him too.

I swung round again and went back to the Ben,
Helping him up to his feet.
Back down in the Grand, he lifted his hand
Toasting the result - a dead heat.

(Jimmy Jardine)

And then in 1975 Cannon made it home first for his fourth victory, twenty seconds outside the record set by Harry Walker in 1973. Walker in fact came in third, behind Mike Short of Horwich RMI Harriers.

Dave Cannon, four times winner in 1976.

175 completed the race with a solo woman runner, Mrs. Joan Glass from Wales, completing the run in 02.17.50. She was not allowed to take part in the official race nand set off some minutes after the men. The mother of three received a special prize from Mrs. Nan MacFarlane.

Race conditions were once again ideal in 1976 when Dave Cannon wrote his name indelibly in the Ben Nevis Race record book. With a BBC team hovering overhead in a helicopter filming the race, Cannon broke all the records, completing the race in 01.26.55, thus becoming the first person to win on five occasions. The race has been won by many great runners, but it is unlikely that Dave Cannon's individual feats will ever be matched.

Scottish Open Hill Championship

BEN NEVIS
RACE 1978

Saturday 2nd September 1978
at 2.30 pm

HRH The Duke of Kent Starting the 1977 Jubilee Race

**From the New Town Park
to the top of Ben Nevis and back   20p**

The Jubilee Race in 1977 saw the first ever Royal presence at the event, with the Duke and Duchess of Kent arriving, accompanied by Lochiel, his son, Donald, and his wife Lady Cecil. The title went to a first-time competitor Alan McGee of Keswick AC, in 01.29.56. The Duke did the honours, presenting him with his gold medal.

He had also acted as starter and met the winners on their return, as did the Duchess. They were particularly interested in 67-year old Norman Bight, a semi-blind runner, who, although banned from the official race, had set off earlier with Kenneth Campbell, a local man, who accompanied him. Bight completed the run in 03.54.00.

Alan MacGee, winner 1977

Mike Davies, still running in 1977

The race was also another milestone in the extraordinary career of Eddie Campbell, who became the first man to receive the Connochie plaque for completing 21 consecutive races. He had, in fact, been participating in his 27th consecutive race.

Eddie Campbell

David Cannon's magnificent achievement in winning his series of races was matched by his effort in gradually reducing the time for the run. His best effort, 01.26.25, came under its greatest threat in 1978 when Billy Bland, Keswick AC, won the race in 01.26.56. Cannon did not run in 1978 as he was abroad representing Britain in a marathon. In second place (for the fourth successive time), came Mike Short, Horwich RMI Harriers, in 01.28.43, the third fastest time ever recorded. Bland was awarded the title of Scottish Open Hill Race Champion, the first time it was awarded in the Ben Race.

Billy Bland, (No 49) 1978 winner

The Ladies' Race was won by Ros Coates, Lochaber AC, in 01.53.23 which was in itself a record as this was the first time an official ladies' event was run. Anne Bland, Kendal AC, was second in 02.07.42 and 3rd Bridget Nogge in 02.07.58 out of a field of 9.

Ros Coates, who dominated the ladies' event in the 70s

Fittingly, in a race in which the record time was subject to the most severe examination, there was a record entry of 362, set on their way by Russell Johnston MP. Eddie Campbell, meanwhile, was still within range of the two hour mark, failing to break the barrier by just 39 seconds, coming in 145th.

The English had dominated the Ben Nevis Race to such an extent that when Colin Donnelly, Clydesdale Harriers, won in 1979, it was the first Scottish victory since 1967. Donnelly had to be treated for blistered feet after his win in 01.31.26. It was his first attempt and he said that he did not expect to win and, indeed, had not set out to do so.

Colin Donnelly, winner, 1979

365 starters (including nine women) had been set off by singer Kenneth McKellar. Billy Bland, Keswick AC, who won in 1978, was third after falling on the hill, and had to be taken to Belford Hospital were 8 stitches were inserted in a cut. Several other runners also ended up in hospital for treatment, but all were discharged by the evening. Ronald Campbell, who came 7th, was the first local, with Ros Coates the first woman, in 81st place.

The late Alister "Scoop" MacMillan, with Race Starter Kenneth McKellar

Ronnie Campbell ("Cammy"), one of Lochaber's most consistent runners in the 1970s.

The celebrations surrounding the first Scottish victory for 13 years were marred by the foolhardy behaviour of three runners who ignored the rules and nearly caused a full scale mountain rescue. Having not even reached the first checkpoint, they failed to inform the organisers that they were withdrawing from the race and were believed to be still on the mountain. They were told by Alister MacIntyre, the Race Committee chairman, that they would not be allowed to take part in the race ever again.

By one of these remarkable co-incidences only sport seems able to conjure up, Ben Nevis won the Grand National at Aintree in 1980, the only year the Ben Race has been cancelled at the start due to adverse weather conditions. A rank outsider ridden by amateur jockey Mr Charles Fenwick, Ben Nevis had not won a race in 12 starts. Only four of the 32 starters in the National finished. Ben Nevis' 13th outing certainly proved lucky (he had made one previous attempt on the National in 1979) while 1980 was a major disappointment for the Ben Race Association.

More history was made in 1980 when, for the first time ever, "Britain's toughest Race" had to be cancelled because of weather conditions. The dramatic moment came when the 400 runners, including 14 women taking part in the first official women's race, were led to the starting line by the Lochaber Junior Pipe Band and awaited the off.

As rain lashed Claggan Park, the athletes sought shelter and the warmth of their track suits, and the loudspeaker blared out that because of a breakdown of the Sno-Trac taking officials on to the mountain the race would not start until 2.30p.m.

Extremely wet and very windy is perhaps understating the conditions at Claggan Park as the summit party struggled to reach the top. Difficulties with the Sno-Trac vehicle which was assisting with the transport of equipment, led to the party being stranded at the half-way point.

A. Gillespie

The half-way point, Saturday, September 6, 1980. Summit Judge Alistair MacLaren and radio-equipped mountain rescue team members could not make it past half-way. Left to right: Alistair Maclaren (time-keeper), Ray Sefton (Team leader, RAF Leuchars), John Hind (Team leader, RAF Kinloss), Donald Watt (with radio, Lochaber Mountain Rescue team).

Meanwhile, at Claggan Park, the failure of the summit party to reach the top was causing concern. Four hundred runners were lining up at the start and eventually the race was postponed for ten minutes. Ben Race Association Chairman Alister MacIntyre was becoming "agitated" according to a report in the January 1981 issue of The Fell Runner. At 2.05pm the delay was extended to another half an hour. Finally, after extensive consultations with medical and mountain rescue personnel, and Race Referee Tom Mackenzie of Inverness, at 2.30pm, the Chairman made the following announcement:

"The police and medical authorities, taking note of conditions on the hill as reported by the mountain rescue, advise us that anyone getting into difficulties would be dead within 25 minutes. Gentlemen, we cannot take that chance with your lives. The 1980 Ben Nevis Race is cancelled."

The 1980 start - " the safety of the runners is always paramount " - Alister MacIntyre.

The runners were predictably outraged at the decision to cancel the race. A request to run on Sunday was refused on the grounds that safety and medical cover could not be organised at short notice. A call for a shorter race was also dismissed.

A number took matters into their own hands however and set off, nine of them, including Eddie Campbell, reaching the top. One says conditions at the summit were "flat calm". While that is treated with some scepticism, there is overwhelming evidence that conditions on the way up were at best treacherous and undoubtedly potentially fatal.

FOR GOD'S SAKE. SLOW DOWN! I'M THE NEXT CHECK-POINT MARSHALL!

Mountain rescue personnel report difficulties in moving equipment to the top and given the vast mountain experience of those who recommended cancelling the race from the position of best possible knowledge - the hill itself - the BNRA appear totally vindicated in their decision to prevent the 400 runners setting off.

The scene mid-way up the Ben

It is estimated that some two-thirds of the runners were inexperienced and while the fell runners may have found conditions less than daunting, the bulk of the field would undoubtedly have been in difficulty. Opinions as to the state of play understandably varied considerably:

John Blair-Fish (Edinburgh Southern): "There is no option but to call it off if the mountain rescue say they cannot rescue. But should they be in a position to say that? If the runners had to carry proper equipment it would perhaps be different."

Colin Donnelly (Cambuslang): "They were quite right to call it off. A lot of inexperienced people do the race and it was so slippy, I am sure there would have been broken limbs."

Ian Holloway (Rochdale): "It was a wise decision, particularly from the casual fell runner's point of view. Obviously I was very disappointed.'

Ken Taylor (Rossendale): "Naturally, I was extremely disappointed, but it was a wise decision. I went up to the Red Burn and it was desperate. But why couldn't they have run to half way or used the next day?"

Harry Jarrett (Cumberland Fell Runners' Association): "I went to half way up and I reckon they should definitely have run the Half-Nevis. It wasn't good enough to do the full Ben, but there was no thought for the runners and their disappointment. I spent over £150 with nothing to show."

Billy Bland (Keswick): "I reckon I would have got up OK, and the other top runners would have been OK. They should have advised us of the situation and left it to us. I just can't see why the mountain rescue couldn't get up."

Alister MacIntyre remains convinced of the propriety of the Race Committee's actions. He said: "The safety of the runners is always paramount and our first priority. While it may be possible for individual runners to reach the top in severe conditions, we have to consider the implications of allowing 400 people to go at one time. It would place an impossible burden on the safety machine if anything was to go wrong. Our expert advice on the hill was to cancel the Race and while that was unfortunate in itself, it was the best and only decision. That way we ensured everyone's safety."

ATHLETICS
ALTERNATIVE TO BEN RACE

The cancellation of last Saturday's Ben Nevis race was a severe blow to the 400 competitors - not least to the eleven entrants from Inverness Harriers, many of whom had travelled to Fort William some time prior to the race to study the ground and had done a lot of specialist training for the event.

Therefore, by way of compensation, Brian Turnbull and Derek McGinn have devised an alternative race which will take place tomorrow (Saturday) from the Bught at 1.30 p.m. Although nowhere near the scale of Ben Nevis, Craig Dunain which many athletes used for training, is the highest there is in the immediate vicinity of Inverness, and a course of 5.3 miles, leading ultimately to the summit, has been worked out. An invitation has been sent to the Ross-shire club to take part as well, and it is hoped that a fairly large field will assemble.

(*Inverness Courier*, Friday, September 12, 1980)

The alternative "Ben Nevis" race up Craig Dunain hill, the week after the ill-fated official event, proved a great success with 21 athletes - mainly from Inverness Harriers but with a few from Ross-shire A.C. and Forres Harriers - taking part. As the event was only conceived a few days earlier, no permit had been applied for and it had to be regarded as an Inverness Harriers club race, with guests taking part as a training run. First home by a fair margin was Brian Turnbull, but after the handicaps had been taken into account, it was Les Hunter, who only joined the club a couple of months previously after a spell as a jogger, who topped the list. In the young athletes' race, Callum Martin had a remarkable run to win from Gary Waite and George MacLennan.

By the time the 1981 race was run, however, there was general satisfaction that safety measures were adequate and that the preparation undertaken for the event would make conditions much more enjoyable for competitors.

There was better luck in store for the runners in 1981, although precious little of it fell the way of winner Robert Whitefield, Kendal AC. He came home in 01.26.57, thirty-two seconds outside David Cannon's best mark.

There were 377 entries with the first full length women's race. Ros Coates excelled and was the first of the Lochaber women home to win in 01.44.25, followed by clubmate, Fiona Wild, with Pauline Haworth, Keswick AC, third.

The balloon literally "went up" on Saturday to mark the start of the 1982 race. As the Long John International balloon rose in the air, the runners were careering round the park having being set off by Mr. D. Campbell of the whisky firm. Billy Bland, Keswick AC, hotly tipped to repeat his success of '81 was among the leaders, but he was hard pressed all the way by Kenneth Stuart. Conditions were perfect as Stuart, the fitter man, came home first in 01.27.12 with Bland second in 01.28.39. Stuart was shown as unattached in the programme but had in fact joined Keswick AC after he had submitted his entry. Robert Whitefield, Kendal AC, was third.

First local was Robert Shields, Lochaber AC, in 6th place in 01.33.14.

Ros Coates, Lochaber AC, was first woman and took the trophy presented by Eddie Campbell who was taking part in his 37th race. Fiona Wild, Lochaber AC, was second. As they checked in each competitor received a whisky miniature, labelled "Ben Nevis Race, 1982".

The first three in 1981 - winner Robert Whitefield in the middle, with Billy Bland on his left and Tacwyn Davies.

Ros Coates again won the women's event in 1983 when the name of Kenneth Stuart, Keswick AC first appeared on the roll of honour. His time of 01.27.12, just seventeen seconds outside the record in his first attempt, gave an indication of his ability and the potential which was eventually to bear fruit two years later.

Two runners were lifted off the mountain by RAF helicopter, one being injured, the other suffering from exhaustion. Eddie Campbell in his 30th race, finished in 01.56.59 and received a specially struck silver medal from the Ben Nevis Race Association, presented by starter John Ligertwood, home sales director of Whyte & MacKay.

BEN RECORD GOES

309 runners set off for the summit, having been set off by Mr. Colin Ross, manager of Ben Nevis Distillery. Minutes after he had smashed the record, Cumberland runner, John Wild said "I was lucky".

He had just knocked 50 seconds off the existing record 01.26.25 set by David Cannon in 1976. In so doing he beat Kenneth Stuart, last year's winner into 2nd place by chasing him and taking a shorter route on the way down.

Shaun Livesey, Clayton-le-Moors Harriers, was 3rd. 1st to the summit was J. Maitland, Aberdeen AC, who took the Lovat Scouts Trophy. Thick mist and rain resulted in several of the runners having to receive first aid and attention at the Belford Hospital.

Officials took the precaution of turning back the competitors who were well behind the scheduled time for the summit.

1st Woman: Ros Coates, Lochaber AC; 1st Local: Ronald Campbell, Lochaber AC. Steve MacLeod in his first race took the Victor Manley Shield for best performance by a local under 23.

(*The Oban Times*, September 8, 1983)

Yet another new record was set in 1984 - the one which stood at the start of the 1994 race - when Ken Stuart, Keswick AC, the hot favourite, won in 01.25.34, one second better than that set by John Wild the previous year. From start to finish Stuart was hard pressed by John Maitland, Aberdeen who was second in 01.26.06 with Hugh Symonds, Kendal AC, third. These three dominated the Race, stretching well away from the rest of the field. Symonds was first to the top, closely followed by Maitland and Stuart. Maitland passed both of them on the last stage from the foot of the mountain, but he was, in turn, passed by Stuart who seemed the fitter.

367 Runners started with Ros Coates' record beaten by Pauline Haworth, Keswick, in 01.45.25. Ros herself came second and Gillian Wilkinson, Keswick, was 3rd.

Ken Stuart, record-breaker, 1984

Pauline Haworth, also a record-breaker.

Nigel Chisholm, Lochaber AC, received his Connochie plaque in the 1984 race, which was the third sponsored by Long John International. Ronnie Campbell, Lochaber AC was 1st local in 15th place. Alister Mac Intyre, Race Committee chairman apologised for the number of runners who had to be disqualified because their entries were received too late, but he criticised the 'unsporting attitude' of the Blackpool runner who won a trophy in 1983, but refused to return it because his entry was too late. He was reported to the English AAA.

Another large field of 445 contested the 1985 race and it was Hugh Symonds, Kendal AC, who won in 1.28.00. Angela Carson, Eryri Harriers, in 01.52.45 was the first woman home in a race run in very good conditions except for snow on the top. There was very little wind, but it was very cold at the summit.

The 1986 race saw the total of runners setting off as near to the 500 mark as possible. 495 started, again in good weather. Colin Donnelly won in 1.25.48, just fourteen seconds short of the record. Angela Carson took the women's prize and England the international trophy. A new name appeared on the first local trophy - (under 23) - D. Mac Gillivray in 01.38.01. The prizes were presented by Mrs. Kathleen MacPherson (Connochie).

Colin Donnelly, winner, 1986, with Kenneth McKellar (left), Duncan MacIntyre (in the glasses) and Donald MacDonald. It was Duncan's last race as he died on July 20, 1987. A tribute in the 1987 Race Programme reminded readers of one incident which summed up his attitude to the race:

On one occasion when the summit party got the Lovat Scouts to radio to base that they doubted if all the members on the top could survive the intense cold for the duration of the race without their ration of Brandy, which had been forgotten. Duncan heard this message - procured two half bottles of Brandy, ran up to the top of the mountain with them, and ran down again in time for the start of the race.

His special place in the history of the race is marked by the award of the Duncan MacIntyre International team trophy, first made in 1985.

Angela Carson, Eryri Harriers

There were 600 entries for the 1987 race and 444 eventually started.

First to the top was Rod Pilbeam, Keswick AC, who was well within the record, but got lost on the way down and ended up coming home 40th.

Mike Lindsay, Carnethy Hill Runners, won in 01.29.25 complete with bruised ribs from the slippery conditions.

Second was Gary Devine, Pudsey & Bramley Harriers, who had dyed his hair magenta to make sure he would be spotted had he got lost. At his first attempt he came home in 01.31.24. Third and fourth were Welsh brothers Hefin and Glyn Griffiths of Eryri Harriers who finished within four minutes of each other.

David Rodgers (20) was the first local home in 8th place. Eight members of Lochaber AC finished in the 1st 40. - D. Rodgers, R. Shields, R. Campbell, D. MacGillivray, S. Fraser, J. MacRae, K. Campbell, D. O' Neill, G. Brooks.

Angela Carson, Eryri Harriers, now wife of Colin Donnelly, the previous year's winner took the women's prize, with Margaret Dunn, Bingley Harriers, second in 02.19.20 and local runner Flora MacNeil third in 02.29.12.

1987 winner - M. Lindsay, Carnethy Hill Runners.

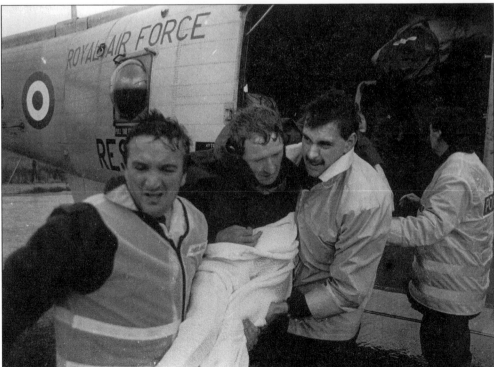

Conditions were desparate in 1988 and the helicopter once again came into its own.

The appalling conditions of 1980 were more than matched in 1988 when disaster was only averted by the sterling work of helicopter crews who ferried runners in difficulties from the hill to Fort William.

Hugh Symonds, Kendal AC, winner in 1985, was one who ran into difficulties. "There were incredibly strong winds and it was very cold. I suffered something which a lot of people had - my eyesight went. It was so cold that your head just wasn't working properly."

Although he was fifth to the summit he finished in 45th position because of his temporary blindness. "It was my worst race ever, but my main concern was getting off the hill alive."

A number of runners were wearing only shorts and singlets despite being warned that conditions were extremely cold. Sixteen were taken to hospital but were released by the evening. There were, fortunately, and perhaps miraculously, no serious injuries.

The winner was Gary Devine, Pudsey & Harriers, who came in 01.30.10, a remarkable time given the conditions. When he set off his hair was dyed a magnificent

1988 Winner Gary Devine, by now minus the punk pink hair!

shade of punk pink; by the time he returned all the dye had been washed out. Sarah Taylor, Horsforth Fellandale was the first woman home in 02.05.23, John Maitland junior the first local. He said he felt he had been able to master the terrible conditions as he worked in the forestry and was accustomed to being outside in all weathers. He was wearing thermals, a woollen hat and gloves. He did find it difficult to keep his feet in places as the gusts of wind were so strong.

Three runners were still unaccounted for as the prize-giving was about to start. Proceedings were delayed until it was confirmed that they were, in fact, wandering around Fort William, not having told anyone they were safe!

The 488 starters had faced the worst weather conditions in 30 years - winds of 70 miles per hour and freezing temperatures. Donald Watt, leader of the Lochaber Mountain Rescue Team, said that he and his members were very close to losing control of the situation. He called on the Race Committee to impose tighter controls on who is allowed to enter the race. He said: "There was no problem with the first 200 runners, but there were far too many fun runners and this not a race for fun runners."

Alister MacIntyre, chairman of the Ben Nevis Race Association, admitted: "It was the worst Ben Nevis Race for the last thirty years. It think it was even worse than in 1980 when it was cancelled."

As a result of events in 1988, the rules for runners were tightened up in 1989. After the fruitless search by five mountain rescue teams and two helicopters for three runners who had not reported their withdrawal from the race delaying the prizegiving, and the number of inexperienced runners who had been overcome by the bad conditions, competitors now had to prove that they were sufficiently experienced to cope, and were instructed to carry a basic survival pack in case they got into trouble. These were to be inspected when runners checked in. The maximum entry was also limited to 500.

1989 - David Rodgers and his clutch of trophies.

1988 Start - Norris Beith of the North British Hotels Trust, sponsors of the 1987, 1988, 1989 and 1990 races.

The 1989 race, started by Norris Beith, was again run in very good conditions. The winner was Keith Anderson (32), Ambleside AC, a chef who was making only his second attempt. He said that his greatest asset in conquering the Ben was the fact that he had slimmed down from thirteen and a half stones to ten and a half. David Rodgers finished fourth overall and took a clutch of local trophies.

David Rodgers with another Ben Nevis legend, Brian Kearney.

Further success followed when the Royal Marine became the first local man to win the race for 34 years in 1991. His time was 01.33.33.

Ros Evans, née Coates, won the the Ladies' Race for the 5th time in 2.03.37. There were 384 starters in brilliant sunshine, the heat causing nine of the competitors to retire.

A year later the title crossed the border once again with twenty-year-old Gavin Bland, an English shepherd from Borrowdale Fell Runners, and nephew of Billy Bland, stole the 1992 Ben Race from David Rodgers by a matter of seconds. Carol Greenwood (Calder Valley Fell Runners) was the first woman home in 01.53.25. Just five of the 351 starters failed to finish and there were 80 newcomers.

Mark Rigby, winner, 1990 (01.26.08) with Keith Anderson (Ambleside AC) who was second on his left, and Gary Devine (Pudsey & Bramley AC), third.

February, 1991 saw the end of an era with the passing of George MacPherson, for many years a distinguished member of the Ben Nevis Race Association. The following was minuted in the Association records (January, 28, 1992):

"George MacPherson has to be given a great deal of the credit for the growth of the Ben Race, during his years as Secretary, when he laid down the pattern that the race was to follow were the foundation on which the Race progressed over the years. George was also family to some a very good friend to others on the Ben Race Committee".

Tribute has often been paid in Race Programmes to the many people who help keep the Ben Race on an even keel on race day. These are the Committee members and helpers who made the 1994 race a successful event, despite some grim weather.

Chapter 8

1991 - 1994
The centenary and the future
It's in my blood

Dear Sir,

In your review of Mr Whymper's contribution to the Leisure Hour for September, in your issue of 28th inst., your reviewer asks the question:- "Is Mr Whymper quite sure that even on a clear day the buildings of Inverness can be seen from the top of Ben-Nevis?"

Perhaps Mr Whymper will not take it amiss if, with your permission, I answer the question.

For some time after we took up our quarters on the Ben, we never missed a good opportunity of exploring the country by eye and telescope with the view of finding what towns &c., could be seen from the summit. In this way we soon discovered we could see Inverness and the sea beyond it.

There is nothing between Inverness and Ben-Nevis to intercept the view, and it is not owing to the distance that the town is more frequently seen from the Ben (for Barra head and the Coast of Ireland, places much more distant, can be seen), but to the fact that even on clear days a cap of smoke hangs over it.

But very early on summer mornings, and best of all on Sunday mornings, when as yet the breakfast fires have not been lighted, the steeples can be seen with the naked eye, while with a good telescope an Invernessian would have no difficulty in recognising the different parts of the town.

I may add that Inverness is the only town visible from the summit of Ben-Nevis.

Yours very truly,
Angus Rankine

(*Inverness Courier*, September 4, 1894)

With David Rodgers heralding the 1990s with a win for Lochaber in 1991, and a promising crop of younger runners threatening to make their mark, the good folk of Lochaber have come to expect a great deal of their local heroes.

The great fell runners of the south still have a major say in the outcome of the Ben Race however and it was a famous name which was engraved on the trophy once again in 1992, Gavin Bland, nephew of former winner Billy, crossing the line in the very fast time of 01.27.02. The twenty-year old Borrowdale Fell Runner has gone on to establish himself as one of the race's most consistent runners of the present era, coming in second to Iain Holmes in 1994.

1992 winner Gavin Bland (third from left) with (left to right) Billy Brooks, David Rodgers and Stephen Burns, all of Lochaber.

One heartening aspect of the 1992 race was the number of newcomers - 145, more than six times the total entry for the 1951 race. The development of the race and its logistical requirements reached new levels of sophistication as well, with up to eighty volunteers deployed on the mountain on race day to oversee the safety of runners, and some thirty deployed in the field itself, before, during and after the race, attending to the welfare of runners and spectators alike.

By now too there were no less than 23 shields, cups and other trophies being awarded, and the race prides itself on being able to provide a full list of finishers with times within three hours of the race ending, as well as engraved medals and signed certificates.

Engraver Alastair McLaren at work.

The 1993 winner was once again a Scot however, Graeme Bartlett of Forres Harriers overcoming difficult conditions - brilliant heat and bright sunshine - to come home in 01.33.38 - eight minutes and four seconds outside the record. Bartlett said: "It was a hard race and I fell two or three times but I kept up and overtook the others on the way down."

Billy Rodgers (left) and Billy Brooks of Lochaber with the local silverware.

Local hero David Rodgers was not a participant as he was competing in the World Hill Running Championships in France. His brother, Billy, got off to a good start and was lying third at the summit. "It was a nightmare, I just died after the summit and couldn't give any more," he said after coming home in 12th position, four places behind John Hepburn, the first local.

Julie Farmer, Leys Mill near Arbroath, competing for the first time, finished in 02.02.18, in 101st place, to take the women's race. "It was very hard in the heat," she said afterwards. "I had a lot of trouble staying on my feet on the way down."

Among the oldest runners in 1993 was 71-year old Jack Riley from Burnley who said it would be his last race. "My wife played hell when she heard I was coming, so this will be the last time," he had said before the race. 346 started the race and 341 completed the run; Mr. Riley was not among them. Nor was he a runner in 1994! Mrs Riley is understood to have played hell indeed!

The 1994 start. Sales of stop-watches have boomed since 1951!

By the time the 1994 race took place, the centenary celebrations had begun and on August 2nd, a special welcome was extended to former runners who took part in a commemorative event organised by Eddie Campbell.

The early morning run, with over 70 participants, took in no less than five previous race starts - from the Leisure Centre at the King George V Park, back into Fort William past one "old Post Office" to another at 88 High Street, then back down the High Street and off to the Ben, up to the summit as usual and back to the Leisure Centre.

The run was jointly sponsored by Lochaber Sports Council and Highland Regional Council and the whole company was treated to a celebratory meal and knees-up in Fort William Shinty Club's splendid new social club at An Aird.

The centenary run was a hugely entertaining event which awoke pleasant memories amongst all concerned. There were many stories told, a few no doubt embellishing others which benefited from the re-telling.

Lochaber Sports Council honoured Eddie Campbell for his contribution to athletics in Lochaber in February, 1994, with a special presentation.

Amongst the participants listed as taking part was the indefatigable Hugo Soper of Vauxhall Motors, with just seven appearances fewer than Eddie Campbell in the full event (36 and 43 respectively including 1994).

The list of runners reads like a Who's Who of Ben Race running - Jimmy Jardine, Alex and Mary Gillespie (who completed a splendid family double), Fiona Wild, John Marstrand, David Love and Harry Swan Young, who was to complete his 21 races qualifying for the Connochie plaque in September.

Jimmy Jardine, as ever, had a word or two set aside to mark the event:

1973 Revisited

Whilst carrying out my employment as a minor civil servant, I was pitched through the plate glass window of MacTavish's Kitchen. Dusting myself off, I felt a bit more disorientated than usual. There at a table sat John Marstrand, Jim Smith and Mike Davies looking just as they did when we all trained up the "Ben" in the weeks before the race. "Jeez Jimmy, what happened to you? You look twenty years older," they chorused. I blurted out "Beware Jim, you're going to have a terrible accident at Moffat and smash both your legs. John you are going to have to retire with groin strain and will devote your life to trying oil extracts from different fish to find a cure to let you do one more "Ben". And Mike, you'll find this hard to believe, but you're going to become dis-solutioned".

"Jimmy, come and sit down," they said, "have you been running in these ultra-violet strips again?" "I come from a time when Eddie has done 42 "Bens", entry is limited to 500, the entry fee is £6 and Eddie no longer wears Green Flash shoes. "Now we know you are kidding," they replied, "the Green Flash shoes give it away."

As the faces, tables and chairs started to dissolve and I was sinking to my knees, I caught a glimpse of the calendar - 1973. Maybe if I could have remained in that time a bit longer, I could have cheered myself on to a medal, but you can't change history. I'll always have been 12th; I'll never have caught up on Martin Weeks and Dave Halstead, the 9th or 10th men who were staggering all over the road from Achintee and Pete Walkington would always have come past me. "I was so near - so, so near," I mumbled.

"Yes, yes, we know," soothing voices said as green overalled arms helped me on to a stretcher, and back out through the window.

The last thing I remember before I passed out was a voice asking if they'd passed. If I didn't get my medal, I'm damn sure they won't get theirs!

Jimmy did get his medal and obviously still has a problem with plate glass windows. He was however, back in his usual place in the 1994 race, which was run in dreadful conditions. In the circumstances, Ian Holmes' winning time of 01.30.17 was a remarkable achievement, with runners being hampered at the summit by the severe cold and rain from start to finish. Billy Rodgers, the first Lochaber man home, in fourth place, upheld the family tradition with brother David once again abroad running in the World Championships and unavailable.

Ian Holmes of Bingley Harriers, winner of the 1994 race in 1 hour 30 minutes 17 seconds. A whirlpool bath fitter (not many of them win the Ben Race!), Ian went to the top in one hour and one minute, suitably fortified by a breakfast of beans on toast.

Second was Gavin Bland of Borrowdale, the 1992 winner, and third his cousin Jonathon, also of Borrowdale. The Blands are nephews of Billy Bland, winner of the race in 1978.

Gill Barnes, Lochaber AC, was first woman home in 1994, in two hours, thirteen minutes and twenty-two seconds. The race was Gill's first, although she had previously done the Half-Ben Race. A native of Cumbria, Gill had recently moved to the Lochaber area, taking up residence in Glen Nevis.

And Hugo Soper was still running, along with Eddie Campbell, clocking up yet another remarkable run. Despite some fairly atrocious weather, there was only one casualty of note, being helicoptered off the Ben. The injured runner (who made a swift recovery), was safely ensconsed in the Belford Hospital before most of the runners returned to Claggan Park.

Rob Cameron and Jean MacDonald kept the crowd entertained and informed as the runners came and went.

The 328 brave souls who braved the elements on September 3, 1994, were following in a long and illustrious tradition of challengers who tackled the mighty Ben. There is a school of thought amongst runners who would like to see the race return to one of its former starting points on the High Street or even Cameron Square.

The logistics and particularly the safety aspects of this would seem to render such a possibility unfortunately inadmissible. While the pedestrianisation of the High Street has much to commend it in terms of spectacle, there is unfortunately no way of accommodating the back-up required at the finish of an event which may now see up to 500 runners taking part.

The weather was at its worst in 1994. There was still some sunshine and Kathleen MacPherson (Connochie) set new standards of elegance!

As to why they all do it, and why many will return to do it again and again - the preceding pages may have gone some way to explaining the reason. George MacFarlane, the redoubtable Ben Race Secretary summed it up thus: *"It is a challenge which is simple, from sea level to the top of our highest mountain and back down again. That's what makes this race unique."*

It may be simple and there is little doubt that the race needs both stamina and courage. In 1994, Eddie Campbell completed his 42nd official race since 1951, a sequence of enormous significance and one which is unlikely ever to be matched. Hugo Soper, at 66, finished for the 35th time. He said: "It was terrible at the top. I've rarely felt so bad up there and it is the first time I've ever stopped to put my waterproof on."

Few competitors epitomise the bravery and fortitude of the Ben Nevis runner better than Eddie and Hugo, legends in their own lifetimes.

The challenge of the race and what it means to competitors cannot be summed up better than in in the words of Fort William bank clerk Nigel Chisholm, who finished last in the 1994 race, exhausted, wet, but still smiling:

"Somehow I do enjoy it, it's in my blood."

A young Nigel Chisholm running in 1960

Ben Nevis *A. Gillespie*

Roll Of Honour

563	St Columba made his epic journey up the Great Glen.
1645	Battle at Inverlochy, Montrose for Charles I defeated Argyll's Covenanters.
1654	*(June)* "Inverlochtie" fort built - site of Fort William.
1692	Massacre of Glencoe.
1735	General Wade's Road from Fort William built.
1746	March 14 - April 3, siege of Fort William.
1773	First emigrant ship left Fort William.
1822	First passage through Caledonian Canal, built by Thomas Telford.
1863	Original Belford Hospital opened.
1870	*(January 28)* Lochaber Curling Club founded - the oldest continuously existing sports club in Lochaber.
1878	Victoria Park opened - later to becomne King George V Park.
1883	Weather observatory built on top of Ben Nevis.
1893	Fort William shinty Club formed.
1894	Traffic commenced on railway from Craigendorran to Fort William (extended to Mallaig thereafter).
1895	*(Sept)* William Swan ran the first timed Ben Nevis Race in 2hrs 41 minutes.
1896	Telegram from summit of Ben Nevis to Queen Victoria (Diamond Jubilee).
1899	Hugh Kennedy runs from the Locheil Arms, Banavie, (2hours 41mins).
1902	Lucy Cameron makes the first woman's timed ascent (2hrs 03mins).
1903	*(Sept)* Ewen MacKenzie establishes record from Post Office (88 High St.), (2hrs 10mins 07secs).
1904	Observatory on summit of Ben Nevis closed.
1908	Fort William shinty Club re-formed.
1909	Miss Wilson-Smith of Duns made a solo attempt on the ascent of Ben Nevis - credited with a time of one hour fifty-one minutes.
1924	Work started on Hydro-electric scheme to generate power for aluminium factory.
1929	Tunnel completed for Hydro-electric scheme; factory declared open.
1932	Fort William Shinty Club re-formed; Kilmallie also formed by now.

1937 *(July)* Charles Wilson, Kilwinning wins the resurrected race
(2hrs 17 mins 52 secs).

MacFarlane Cup presented by Mr G. MacFarlane, later Provost of
Fort William.

1939 D. Mulholland, Ardeer establishes record from Post Ofice (88 High Street),
2hrs 03 mins 43secs.

1942 *(May)* Duncan MacIntyre collapses within sight of the line, leading the race.
Wilson wins for third time.

1943 *(June)* First race from King George V Park. Duncan MacIntyre wins in
2hrs 04 mins 30secs.

1945 Peace cairn erected on summit of Ben Nevis.

1946 Lochaber Camanachd formed - amalgamation of Brae Lochaber and Spean
Bridge.

1951 *(August)* Brian Kearney, Fort William wins, breaking two hours for the first
time -1hr 51mins 18secs.

1952 *(June)* Eddie Campbell, Fort William wins his first race in
01hr 53 mins 46 secs.

1955 *September 3* - 16-year old Kathleen Connochie made her famous solo run to
the top of Ben Nevis, accompanied by Duncan MacIntyre. She completed the
run (from the King George V Park to the top and back) in 3hrs 2mins.
Duncan was a record holder of the Ben Race from the King George Park,
winning in 1943. The race was dominated in the fifties by St Mary's Athletic
Club members Eddie Campbell and Brian Kearney, who won the race three
times each. Eddie and Brian won the 1954 team race, along with D. I. Dando.

1956 MacAulay Cup Final - Kyles Athletic 2 Fort William:
Fort William's first senior shinty championship.

1957 John Rix dies on Ben Nevis - the only recorded fatality in the race.

1958 *(Sept)* D. A. Spencer, Barrow, wins first of three consecutive races in
1hr 46 mins 08 secs. First person to complete hat-trick.

1961 First Camanachd Cup Final at King George V Park, Fort William -
Kingussie 2 Oban Celtic 1.

1962 *(Sept)* Peter Hall, Barrow, wins the first of his four successive races in
1hr 45mins 44secs. Only man to do four in a row.

1964 Camanachd Cup Final at King George V Park - Kilmallie 4 Inveraray 1.

1965 New Belford Hospital opened by HRH Princess Margaret.

1968 Last sports gathering at King George V Park before swimming pool built.

1969 Lochaber Rugby Club founded.

1971 *(Sept)* David Cannon wins first of his five races in six years in
1hr 33mins 05secs. First race from Claggan Park.

1973 Swimming pool built on King George V Park.

1974 Fort William FC formed.

1975 Fort William Town Council formed on local government re-organisation.

1978 *(Sept)* Ros Coates, Lochaber AC, wins first women's race of modern era in
1hr 49 mins 22 secs.

1980 Ben Nevis Race cancelled as runners prepared to set off, due to atrocious
weather conditions.

1982 *(Sept)* Women admitted as "official" participants in Ben Nevis Race.

1984 *(Sept)* Kenneth Stuart, Keswick AC, establishes new record for men - 1hr 25
mins 34 secs.

Pauline Haworth establishes modern record for women - 1hr 43 mins 25 secs.

1985 New record entry of 500 for Ben Nevis Race.

1985 *(August 7)* Fort William FC win first match in Highland League, versus
Clach (1-0) at home.

1992 Camanachd Cup Final - Fort William 1 Kingussie 0 at Glasgow.

1994 History of Fort William Shinty Club published.

History of the Ben Nevis Race published.

Jimmy Jardine's view of the Centenary Run turn at the Post Office (left), August 2, 1994. Kathleen MacPherson (Connochie) acted as the turning point!

The Ben Race

Winning times 1895 ~ 1994

If at first you don't succeed, try again;
Mist and rain you should not heed, try again;
When the clouds have rolled away,
And the sun holds glorious sway,
Climb the path without delay, come again,
All your favours he'll repay - grand old Ben.

(Observatory Visitors' Book)

(Abbreviations: **OPO** - Original Post Office; **LA** - Locheil Arms; **NPO** - New Post Office (88 High Street); **KGV** - King George V Park; **CP** - Claggan Park)
★ denotes unbeaten record

Date		Start	Winner	Time
1895	**September**	**OPO**	**William Swan, Fort William**	**2.41.00 ★**
1897		NPO	Col. Spencer Acklom	2.55.00
1898	Aug 2	NPO	William MacDonald, Leith	2.27.00
		NPO	T.J.S. Hunter, Edinburgh	2.33.00
	Oct 29	NPO	W. Swan, Fort William	2.20.00
1899	June 3	LA	Hugh Kennedy, Banavie	02.41.00★
	June 3	LA	W. MacDonald, Leith	03.13.00
	Aug 29	NPO	W. MacDonald, Leith	02.18.00
1902		NPO	Lucy Cameron, Ardechive	02.03.00 (ascent)
	July 19	NPO	Elizabeth Tait, Spean Bridge	01.59.30 (ascent)
1903	Sept 28	NPO	E. MacKenzie, Fort William	02.10.06
	Sept 28	NPO	H. Kennedy, Banavie	02.12.22

1909	Sept 14	NPO	Elizabeth Wilson-Smith, Duns	01.51.00 ★(ascent)
1937	July 20	NPO	C.P. (Charles) Wilson, Kilwinning	02.17.52
1938	June 28	NPO	C.P. Wilson, Kilwinning	02.13.30
1939	**July 17**	**NPO**	**D. Mulholland, Ardeer**	**02.03.43★**
	July 1	NPO	Mike Reavey, Fort William	02.05.30
1942	May 20	NPO	C.P. Wilson, Kilwinning	02.25.49
1943	June 23	KGV	Duncan MacIntyre, Fort William	02.04.30
1944	June 21	KGV	C.P. Wilson, Kilwinning	02.14.19
1951	Aug 15	KGV	Brian C. Kearney, Fort William	01.51.18
1952	June 18	KGV	Eddie Campbell, Fort William	01.53.46
1953	July 25	KGV	Eddie Campbell, Fort William	01.53.18
1954	**June 26**	**KGV**	**Brian Kearney, Fort William**	**01.47.04★**
1955	Sept 3	KGV	Eddie Campbell, Fort William	01.50.05
	Sept 3	**KGV**	**Kathleen Connochie, Fort William**	**03.02.00 ★**
1956	Sept 1	KGV	Pat Moy, Vale of Leven	01.45.55
1957	Sept 7	KGV	Brian Kearney, Fort William	01.46.04
1958	Sept 6	KGV	David A. Spencer, Barrow	01.46.08
1959	Sept 5	KGV	D. A. Spencer, Barrow	01.47.53
1960	Sept 3	KGV	D. A. Spencer, Barrow	01.52.22
1961	Sept 2	KGV	Michael P. Davies, Reading	01.47.56
1962	Sept 1	KGV	Peter Hall, Barrow	01.45.44
1963	Sept 7	KGV	Peter Hall, Barrow	01.41.45
1964	**Sept 5**	**KGV**	**Peter Hall, Barrow**	**01.38.50★**
1965	Sept 4	KGV	Peter Hall, Barrow	01.42.19
1966	Sept 3	KGV	Allan MacRae, Lochaber AC	01.43.49
1967	Sept 2	KGV	R. Shields Clydesdale H	01.41.11
1968	Sept 7	KGV	M. P. Davies, Reading AC	01.39.29
1969	Sept 6	KGV	M. P. Davies, Reading AC	01.43.25
1970	Sept 5	KGV	J. Norman, Altrincham & District	01.40.45
1971	Sept 4	NTP	David Cannon, Kendal AC	01.33.05
1972	Sept 2	NTP	David Cannon, Kendal AC	01.32.57
1973	Sept 1	NTP	H.D. Walker, Blackburn Harriers	01.29.38
1974	Sept 7	NTP	David Cannon, Kendal AC	01.30.17
1975	Sept 6	NTP	David Cannon, Kendal AC	01.29.58

1976	Sept 4	NTP	David Cannon, Gateshead AC	01.26.25
1977	Sept 3	NTP	Allan MacGee, Keswick AC	01.29.56
1978	Sept 2	NTP	William Bland, Keswick AC	01.26.56
1978	Sept 2	NTP	Ros Coates, Lochaber AC	01.53.23
1979	Sept 1	NTP	Colin Donnelly, Cambuslang H.	01.31.26
1980	September	**RACE CANCELLED**		
1981	Sept 5	NTP	Robert Whitefield, Kendal AC	01.26.57
	Sept 5	NTP	Ros Coates, Lochaber AC	01.44.25
1982	Sept 4	NTP	Kenneth Stuart, Keswick AC	01.27.12
	Sept 4	NTP	Ros Coates, Lochaber AC	01.49.22
1983	Sept 3	NTP	John R. Wild, Cumberland FR	01.25.35
	Sept 3	NTP	Ros Coates, Lochaber AC	01.45.17
1984	**Sept 1**	**NTP**	**Kenneth Stuart, Keswick AC**	**01.25.34★**
	Sept 1	**NTP**	**Pauline Haworth, Keswick AAC**	**01.43.25★**
1985	Sept 7	NTP	H. Symonds, Kendal AC	01.28.00
	Sept 7	NTP	Angela Carson, Rhedwr Eryri	01.52.45
1986	Sept 6	NTP	C.K. Donnelly, Eryri Harriers	01.25.48
	Sept 6	NTP	Angela Carson, Rhedwr Eryri	01.47.51
1987	Sept 5	NTP	M. Lindsay, Carnethy Hill Runners	01.29.25
	Sept 5	NTP	Angela Carson, Rhedwr Eryri	01.52.57
1988	Sept 2	NTP	G. Devine, Pudsey and Bramley AC	01.30.10
	Sept 2	NTP	Sara Taylor, Horsforth Fellandale	02.05.23
1989	Sept 2	NTP	Keith Anderson, Ambleside AC	01.27.41
	Sept 2	NTP	Beverley Redfern, Carnethy H. R.	02.03.10
1990	Sept 1	NTP	Mark Rigby, Westerlands CCC	01.26.08
	Sept 1	NTP	Lesley Hope, Lochaber AC	01.56.58
1991	Sept 7	NTP	David Rodgers, Lochaber AC	01.33.33
	Sept 7	NTP	Ros Evans, Lochaber AC	02.03.57
1992	Sept 6	NTP	Gavin Bland, Borrowdale FR	01.27.02
	Sept 6	NTP	Carol Greenwood, Calder Valley FR	01.53.25
1993	Sept 4	NTP	Graeme Bartlett, Forres Harriers	01.33.38
	Sept 4	NTP	Julie Farmer, Lochaber AC	02.02.18
1994	Sept 3	NTP	Ian Holmes, Bingley Harriers & AC	01.30.17
	Sept 3	NTP	Gill Barnes, Lochaber AC	02.13.22

BEN NEVIS
RACES 1951-60

Ten years

by Eddie Campbell

Souvenir Booklet

1951 - 1960

The Golden Era

"The challenge of Ben Nevis is for ever there for all to see"
With grateful thanks to Eddie Campbell

RACE RESULTS
1951
Wednesday, 15th August at 3pm from King George V Park.
Race starter, Ex-Provost Mr George MacFarlane

			Hrs	Mins	Secs
1.	**Brian C. Kearney**	**Fort William**	1	51	18
2.	Eddie Campbell	Fort William	1	56	35
3.	Tommy Kearney	Fort William	2	9	18
4.	Duncan Macintyre	Fort William	2	10	55
	Farquhar MacRae	Lochailort	2	16	
	A. MacDonald ('Wallace')	Fort William	2	27	
	Charlie Sim.	Fort William	2	29	
	Allan Petrie	Annat	2	35	35
	H. R. Phillip.	Edinburgh			
	A. Harper	Inverness			
	Allan Grant	Tomdoun			
	A. D. N. Breckenridge	Glasgow			
	Allan MacLean	Fort William		Also ran	
	Archie MacLachlan	Fort William		Times mislaid	
	A. MacKenzie	Glenurquhart			
	C. Petrie. (Charlie)	Annat			
	F. W. Doswell. R.N. Base	Glasgow			
	J. Scullion R.N. Base	Glasgow			
	Jock Petrie	Annat			
	C. Mathieson	Ardlui		Retired	
	T. Byford	Fort William			

A new record, with the two-hour barrier broken

1952

Wednesday 18th June at 3pm. From King George V Park.
Race starter - Mr Duncan MacIntyre.
Team trophy for annual competition presented by Mrs J. W. Hobbs.

			Hrs	*Mins*	*Secs*
1.	**E. Campbell**	**Fort William**	**1**	**53**	**46**
2.	C. Petrie	Fort William	1	55	45
3.	J. Conn	Fort William	2	8	22
4.	J. Miller	Dundee	2	8	27
5.	M. Notman	Inverness	2	11	27
6.	A. Petrie	Fort William	2	14	
7.	F. MacRae	Lochailort	2	14	20
8.	A. MacDonald	Fort William	2	17	30
9.	M. Nicholson	Portree	2	18	35
10.	J. Harper	Inverness	2	25	17
11.	A. Roberts	Inverlochy	2	25	45
12.	A. MacLean	Fort William	2	28	35
13.	A. Sutherland	Inverness	2	31	24
14.	H. R. Phillip	Aberdeen	2	34	45
15.	J. R. Scott	Glasgow	2	58	45
	W. Howie	Clydebank			
	J. Scullion	Govan			
	A. Watson	Govan			
	J. Traynor	Govan			
	J. Walker	Govan		— Retired	
	D. Love	Fort William			
	A. MacLachlan	Fort William			
	L. Munday	Maryhill			
	A. Erray	Kent			

New team trophy - won for the first time by the Ben Nevis Athletic Club - Charlie Petrie (or "Chuck" as he is now know in Canada), Jimmy Conn and Allan Petrie. Winner Eddie Campbell had never seen such atrocious conditions at the top of Ben Nevis.

1953

Saturday 25th July at 4.30pm. From King George V Park.

Race Starter - Jock Petrie set the runners off with a double-barrel shotgun, which all runners made sure he was pointing upwards!

	Name	Club	Hrs	Mins	Secs
1.	**E. Campbell**	**Fort William**	1	53	18
2.	D.I. Dando	Glasgow	2	-	25
3.	A. Fleming	Glasgow	2	3	53
4.	J. Conn	Fort William	2	4	42
5.	H. R. Phillip	Edinburgh	2	5	16
6.	C. Petrie	Fort William	2	6	55
7.	A. MacDonald	Fort William	2	10	59
8.	J. Miller	Dundee	2	11	45
9.	J. Sellers	Paisley	2	18	40
10.	A. Petrie	Fort William	2	21	35
11.	R. McDermott	Glasgow	2	30	45
12.	J. Simpson	Kinlochleven	2	34	40
13.	D. Love	Fort William	2	35	-
14.	J. Allison	Bishopbriggs	2	35	30
15.	W. Howie	Clydebank	2	38	45
16.	J. Duffy	Clydebank	2	40	30
17.	C. Kirk	Glasgow	2	46	39
18.	H. Clarke	Glasgow	2	49	-
19.	J. Scott	Glasgow	2	58	19
	J. Shields	Glasgow	Retired		

Team trophy

	Team	Members	Points
1.	Lochaber Sports	(Campbell, Dando, Simpson)	15
2.	Ben Nevis Athletic	(Conn, Petrie, MacDonald)	17
3.	Glasgow and District	(Fleming, Sellers, McDermott)	23
4.	Clydesdale and Bellahouston.		
5.	Y.M.C.A. Glasgow		

1954
Saturday 26th June at 4.30pm from King George V Park
Race Starter - Major Hume

			Hrs	Min	Sec
1.	**B. Kearney**	**Fort William**	**1**	**47**	**4**
2.	E. Campbell	Fort William	1	49	9
3.	W. Gallacher	Glasgow	1	54	41
4.	D.I. Dando	Fort William	1	56	15
5.	J. Conn	Fort William	1	56	32
6.	A. MacDonald	Fort William	2	5	2
7.	J. Timmins	Dumbarton	2	12	14
8.	T. Kearney	Fort William	2	13	56
9.	F. Kielty	Glasgow	2	16	34
10	B. Armstrong	Glasgow	2	17	20
11.	A. Fleming	Glasgow	2	19	50
12	J. M. Sellers	Paisley	2	19	52
13.	D. M. Bowman	Glasgow	2	22	35
14.	A. McEachern	Fort William	2	27	35
15.	J. Geddes	Glasgow	2	30	48
16.	W. Howie	Glasgow	2	31	41
17.	A. MacLean	Fort William	2	34	55
18	J. McEachern	Glasgow	2	38	57
	J. R. Scott,	Glasgow		Finished together	
	D. McQueen	Glasgow		- no times taken	
	T. Nisbett	Bishopbriggs			
	D. Love	Fort William			
	H. Howard	Glasgow		Retired	
	N. Cotter	Cambridge			

Team Trophy

		Points
1.	St Mary's Fort William (Kearney, Campbell, Dando)	7
2.	Glasgow and District (Timmins, Sellers, Geddes.)	34
3.	Clydesdale Harriers (Kielty, Bowman, Howie.)	38

1955
Saturday 3rd September at 3.30pm
From King George V Park
Race Starter - Mr J. Thompson

			Hrs	*Min*	*Sec*
1.	**E. Campbell,**	**Fort William**	**1**	**50**	**5**
2.	J. Hand	Carlisle	2	1	59
3.	A. Hume	Fersit	2	3	4
4.	D.L. Thomson	Tighnabruaich	2	6	50
5.	J. Timmins	Dumbarton	2	7	35
6.	R. Shaw	Carlisle	2	8	58
7.	P. Moy	Vale of Leven	2	9	33
8.	S. Horn	Glasgow	2	9	54
9.	R.H. Wilson	Bellahouston	2	10	11
10.	P. Wright	Tulloch	2	12	5
11.	J. Conn	Fort William	2	12	43
12.	J. Hume	Glasgow	2	14	59
13.	R. A. Sinclair	Falkirk	2	19	40
14.	D. Love	Fort William	2	27	55
15.	F. Kielty	Glasgow	2	28	39
16.	T. Rowcastle	Glasgow	2	29	28
17.	R. Boyd	Glasgow	2	30	38
18.	A. H. Fleming	Cambuslang	2	31	38
19.	G. Boyd	Glasgow	2	39	38
20.	J. Bethel	Glasgow	2	39	38
21.	A. MacLean	Fort William	2	48	25
22.	J. J. Hewitt	Cambridge	2	51	50
23.	J. McEachern	Shettleston	2	53	52
24.	A. Cook	Falkirk	2	56	22
25.	J. R. Scott	Glasgow	3	6	59
26.	D. McQueen	Shettleston	3	7	45
	G. Calder	Inverness	Retired		

Team Trophy   **Points**

1.	Glasgow and District "B"	(Timmins, Moy, Horn)	20
2.	"England"	(Hand, Shaw, Hewitt)	30
3.	Clydesdale Harriers	(Hume, Kielty, Boyd)	35
4.	Glasgow and District "A"	(Wilson, McEachern, McQueen)	58
5.	Glasgow and District "C"	(Rowcastle, Bethel, Scott)	61

Team trophy taken out of Fort William for the first time. The Ben Nevis Race Association had been formed- President Mr George MacFarlane. Having been banned from the race, Kathleen Connochie completed a solo run in 3 hours and 2 minutes.

1956
Saturday 1st September at 3 30pm from King George V Park
Race Starter - Mr J. Thompson

			Hrs	Mins	Secs
1.	**P. Moy**	**Vale of Leven A.A.C.**	1	45	55
2.	S. Horn	Garscube Harriers	]	48	59
3.	E. Campbell	St Mary's, Fort William	1	49	0
4.	B.C. Kearney	St Mary's, Fort William	1	55	2
5.	J. Bushby	Clayton le Moors Harriers	1	57	0
6.	J. Hand	Border Harriers, Carlisle	1	58	0
7.	J. Conn	Ben Nevis Race Association	2	0	55
8.	R.H. Wilson	Bellahouston Harriers	2	1	30
9.	W. Lawrence	Elgin A.C.	2	1	30
10.	A. Hume	Ben Nevis Race Association	2	2	40
11.	A. Kidd	Garscube Harriers	2	2	45
12.	C. H. Taylor	Ben Nevis Race Association	2	4	15
13.	J. Linn	Garscube Harriers	2	4	35
14.	J. Timmins	Dumbarton A.A.C.	2	4	45
15.	D.L. Thomson	Bute Shinty A.C.	2	6	48
16.	A. Heaton	Clayton-le-Moors H., Burnley	2	9	32
17.	C.W. Foley	Pitreavie A.C. Dunfermline	2	12	45
18.	A. MacLean	St Mary's, Fort William	2	12	55
19.	S. Bradshaw	Clayton-le-Moors H., Burnley	2	13	0
20.	J.G. McLean	Bellahouston Harriers	2	17	0
21.	F. Kielty	Clydesdale Harriers	2	17	30
22	D.M. Bowman	Clydesdale Harriers	2	17	30
23	W. Charnley	Clayton-le-Moors H., Burnley	2	18	50
24.	K. Heaton	Clayton-le-Moors H., Burnley	2	18	51
25	I.C. Grainger	Edinburgh Southern Harriers	2	19	10
26.	P.D. Wright	Ben Nevis Race Association	2	19	15
27.	R.A. Sinclair	Falkirk Victoria Harriers	2	19	28
28.	E. MacDonald	St. Mary's, Fort William	2	20	0
29.	R. Shaw	Border Harriers, Carlisle	2	22	0
30.	B. Lister	Clayton-le-Moors H., Burnley	2	22	30
31.	D.G.W. Nichol	Falkirk Victoria Harriers	2	25	0
32.	J. Bethell	Unattached, Glasgow	2	28	30
33.	J. Welshman	Pitreavie A.C. Dunfermline	2	30	0
34.	A. L. Byers	Border Harriers, Carlisle	2	30	
35.	A. Fleming	Cambuslang Harriers	2	35	55
36.	E.G. Dunster	Elgin A.C.	2	36	0
37.	R.J. Clarke	Glenmore Sports Club, Aviemore	2	40	0

38.	J. Bray	Pitreavie A. C. Dunfermline	2	41	10
39	R.H. McDermott	Babcock & Wilcox A.C.	2	41	15
40	M.B. Denver	Pitreavie A.C., Dunfermline	2	44	0
41.	D. McQueen	Shettleston Harriers	2	44	0
42.	G. Bell	Bellahouston Harriers	2	53	0
43.	G. Seabrook	Pitreavie A.C., Dunfermline	2	55	0
44.	J. Boyd	Clydesdale Harriers	2	58	0
45.	M. Stagg	Unattached, Hornchurch, Essex	3	6	0
46.	H. Cameron	Unattached, Fort William	3	6	0
47.	Corp. McLeod	R.M.F.V.R. Govan	3	20	0
48.	A. Cook	Falkirk Victoria Harriers	3	22	0
49.	J. Mulrooney	Cambuslang Harriers	3	24	0
50.	A. Reid	Springburn Harriers	3	30	0
51.	Marine Gourley	R.M.F.V.R. Govan	3	46	0
52.	Marine Lamb	R.M.F.V.R. Govan	3	50	0
53.	Marine McKelvie	R.M.F.V.R. Govan	3	50	0

Team Trophy   **Points**

1.	Lochaber & District "A".	(Campbell, Kearney, Conn)	14
2.	Garscube Harriers.	(Horn, Kidd, Linn)	26
3.	Clayton-le-Moors H. "B".	(Bushby, Bradshaw, Charnley)	47
4.	Glasgow & District "B".	(Moy, Timmins, Fleming)	50
5.	Lochaber & District "B".	(Taylor, MacLean, Wright)	56
6.	Border Harriers, Carlisle.	(Hand, Shaw, Byers)	69
	(Joint) Bellahouston Harriers.	(Wilson, McLean, Bell)	70
7.	Clayton-le-Moors H. "A".	(Heaton (A), Heaton (K), Lister)	70
8.	Clydesdale Harriers.	(Kielty, Bowman, Boyd)	87
9.	Pitreavie A. C. Dunfermline.	(Foley, Welshman, Bray)	88
10.	Falkirk Victoria Harriers.	(Sinclair, Nichol, Cook)	106
11.	Glasgow & District "C".	(McQueen, Bethell, McDermott)	112
12.	R.M.F.V.R. Govan.	MacLeod, Gourley, Lamb)	150

Weather conditions perfect. Visibility unlimited. A new race record.

1957

Saturday 7th September at 3.30pm from King George V Park

Race starter - Mr Chris Brasher (of Olympic Fame)

			Hrs	*Mins*	*Secs*
1.	**B. Kearney**	**Lochaber**	**1**	**46**	**4**
2.	N.G. Addison	Unattached (lst Visitor)	1	54	13
3.	D.A. Spencer	Barrow	1	54	37
4.	E. Campbell	Lochaber (lst Local)	1	55	30
5.	F. Dawson	Salford	1	56	32
6.	A. Hume	Lochaber	1	57	4
7.	D. Thomson	Bute	2	0	50
8.	C.W. Foley	Pitreavie	2	0	59
9.	A.G. Nowell	Waterloo	2	1	23
10.	E. Beard	Leeds	2	1	38
11.	W.F. Lindsay	Edinburgh S.	2	1	39
12.	J. Hand	Border	2	2	32
13.	A. Heaton	Clayton	2	3	27
14.	J. Conn	Lochaber	2	3	32
15.	J. Linn	Garscube	2	4	29
16.	S. Horn	Garscube	2	6	13
17.	R. Cotton	Rotherham	2	6	34
18.	D. S. Pearson	Leeds	2	6	48
19.	G. Eadie	Cambuslang	2	7	56
20.	W. Lawrence	Elgin	2	8	11
21.	P. Dugdale	Clayton	2	8	58
22.	F. Barnfield	Leeds	2	9	43
23.	W. Shearer	R.A.F.	2	9	59
24.	W. Charnley	Clayton	2	11	38
25.	W. Curran	Edinburgh S.	2	11	53
26.	J. Goulding	Edinburgh S.	2	12	33
27.	R.H. Wilson	Bellahouston	2	12	46
28.	A.H. Fleming	Cambuslang	2	12	49
29.	J. Bruce	Edinburgh S.	2	13	13
30.	B. Lister	Clayton	2	15	11
31.	G. Bradshaw	Benwell	2	16	11
32.	K. Borthwick	Edinburgh S.	2	16	45
33.	K. Heaton	Clayton	2	17	12
34.	W. Kelly	Cambuslang	2	17	45
35.	S. Bradshaw	Clayton (lst Veteran)	2	18	23
36.	A. Byers	Border	2	19	14
37.	B.F. Linn	Garscube	2	19	15
38.	D. Bowman	Clydesdale	2	20	17
39.	M. Moan	Lochaber	2	21	2
40.	A. P. Hickson	Leeds	2	21	48
41.	J. C. Fleming-Smith	Rotherham	2	22	31
42.	R. Birkinshaw	Rotherham	2	22	41
43.	M. Whiteoak	Clayton	2	23	16
44.	J. Timmins	Dumbarton	2	25	37
45.	H. Cameron	Lochaber	2	26	2
46.	I. C. Grainger	Edinburgh	2	26	47

47.	J. Welshman	Pitreavie	2	28	39
48.	M.R. Sawyer	Swindon	2	29	45
49.	D. Marney	Unattached	2	31	3
50.	R. Miquel	Bellahouston	2	32	10
51.	J. Bethell	Hutcheson	2	32	16
52.	H. Fox	Shettleston	2	35	12
53.	G. Jennings	Shaftesbury	2	37	24
54.	C. Taylor	Lochaber	2	37	54
55.	G.D. Thornton	Leeds S.M.	2	44	8
56.	T.N. Ambrose	Liverpool P.	2	46	52
57.	D.A. Cox	Southampton U.	2	52	8
58.	J.M. Sellars	Paisley	2	52	11
59.	J. Geddes	Monkland	2	52	46
60.	S. Lee	Vegetarian	2	54	18
61.	G.S. Pearson	Coventry G.	2	56	23
62.	J. Munkman	Leeds	3	3	46
63.	G. Seabrook	Pitreavie	3	9	18
64.	D.G. Barker	Leeds H.	Time not taken		
65.	J. M. S. Dodd	Forres	Time not taken		
66.	R. W. Howell	Polytechnic	Time not taken		
67.	A. MacLean	Lochaber	Retired		
68.	D. Love	Lochaber	Retired		
69.	A. P. Stone	Orpington	Retired		
70.	M. P. S. Tulloh	Southampton	Retired		
71.	D. McQueen	Shettleston	Retired		
72.	J. C. Jewell	South London	Retired		
73.	J. MacEachern	Shettleston	Retired		
74.	J. Macinally	Dundee	Retired		
75.	J Petrie	Dundee	Retired		
76.	J Rix		Retired		

Team Trophy — **Points**

1.	Lochaber Athletic Club "A".	(Campbell, Hume, Kearney)	11
2.	Leeds Athletic Club.	(Barnfield, Beard, Pearson)	50
3.	Clayton-le-Moors "A".	(Charnley, Dugdale, Heaton)	58
4.	Edinburgh Southern H.	(Bruce, Curran, Lindsay)	65
5.	Garscube Harriers.	(Horn, B. Linn, J. Linn)	68
6.	Cambuslang Harriers.	(Eadie, Fleming, Kelly)	81
7.	Rotherham Athletic Club.	(Birkinshaw, Cotton, Fleming-Smith)	100
8.	Clayton-le-Moors "B".	(Bradshaw, Lister, Whiteoak)	108
9.	Pitreavie Athletic Club.	(Foley, Seabrook, Welshman)	118
10.	Lochaber Athletic Club "B".	(Cameron, Moan, Taylor)	138

The newly formed Lochaber Athletic team had the first and last team. John Rix died on the hill, the only fatality recorded during a race.

1958

Saturday 6th September at 2.30pm from King George V Park

Race Starter - Mr Malcolm McCulloch C.B.E., D.L. Chief Constable, City of Glasgow Police.

			Hrs	*Mins*	*Secs*
1.	**D.A. Spencer**	**Barrow A.C.**	**1**	**46**	**8**
2.	F. Dawson	Salford H. (1st Visitor)	1	48	57
3.	P. Moy	Vale of Leven	1	50	53
4.	J. Conn	Lochaber A.C. (1st Local)	1	52	05
5	E. Campbell	Lochaber A.C.	1	53	33
6	H. Clayton	Wakefield H. (1st Newcomer)	1	56	32
7.	J. McCormick	Springburn H.	1	56	58
8.	E. Sinclair	Springburn H.	1	57	30
9.	G. Rhodes	North Staffs. H.	1	58	32
10.	W. Lawrence	Forres H.	1	59	01
11.	D.S. Pearson	Leeds A.C.	1	59	55
12.	W.A. Lindsay	Pitreavie A.C.	2	0	57
13.	C.W. Foley	Pitreavie A.C.	2	2	49
14.	J. Linn	Garscube H.	2	3	23
15.	A.A. Robertson	Reading A.C. (1st Veteran)	2	4	17
16.	D.L. Thomson	Lochaber A.C.	2	5	6
17.	G. Thornton	Leeds St. Marks	2	5	22
18.	R.H. Wilson	Bellahouston H.	2	5	54
19.	W. Jamieson	Plebian H.	2	5	59
20.	E. MacDonald	Lochaber A.C.	2	6	59
21.	G. Eadie	Cambuslang H.	2	7	9
22.	P. Blackburn	Unattached	2	7	36
23.	W.F. Lindsay	Edinburgh Southern H.	2	7	48
24.	M. Logie	Springburn H.	2	9	7
25.	M. Moan	Lochaber A.C.	2	12	29
26.	W.J. Kelly	Cambuslang H.	2	12	45
27.	J.E. Welshman	Pitreavie A. C.	2	12	51
28.	H. Cameron	Lochaber A.C.	2	13	16
29.	H. Thompson	Rotherham H.	2	14	11
30.	S. Bradshaw	Clayton-le-Moor H.	2	15	17
31.	W.H. Wilson	Garscube H.	2	15	19
32.	J. McLean	Bellahouston H.	2	15	29
33.	J.C. Fleming-Smith	Rotherham H.	2	17	21
34.	J B. Barnard	Ealing H.	2	18	33
35.	D.C. Case	Ealing H.	2	19	24
36.	M. Boylen	Vauxhall Motors A.C.	2	19	57
37.	C. P. Grundy	Salford H.	2	20	38
38.	D. G. Barker	Leeds Harehill H.	2	21	10
39.	G. Jennings	Shaftsbury H.	2	21	18
40.	D. Smith	Wakefield H.	2	27	59.
41.	D.M. Bowman	Clydesdale H.	2	28	54
42.	J. Jacobs	Springburn H.	2	29	
43.	C. L. Taylor	Lochaber A.C.	2	29	36
44.	I. A. Allison	Rotherham H.	2	30	31
45.	D. Wilmoth	Springburn H.	2	31	48
46.	A. Fleming	Cambuslang H.	2	31	56

47.	H. Soper	Vauxhall Motors A.C.	2	32	27
48.	D. Large	Barrow A.C.	2	32	42
49.	T. Mercer	Bellahouston H.	2	32	47
50.	R. McCulloch	Springburn H.	2	33	15
51.	B. Birkinshaw	Rotherham H.	2	34	3
52.	M. Blackwell	Cambridge A.C.	2	34	54
53.	I.C.J. Grainger	Edinburgh Southern H.	2	35	12
54.	E.J. Vine	Maidstone H.	2	36	11
55.	R. Wilson	Wolverhampton H.	2	36	28
56.	D.M. Sutcliffe	St. Alban City A.C.	2	39	44
57.	J. Geddes	Monkland H.	2	39	56
58.	B. Smethurst	Plebian H.	2	40	57
59.	B. Marshland	Wakefield H.	2	48	12
60.	G.E. Seabrook	Vauxhall Motors A.C.	2	50	28
61.	W. Hunter	Lochaber A.C.	2	54	4
62.	W. Coates	Belgrave H.	2	56	48
63.	A.L. Winter	Ranleigh H.	2	58	11
64.	D. McQueen	Shettleston H.	2	59	28
65.	J.S.C. Hume	R.A.F. Buchan	2	59	28
66.	A. Reid	Springburn H.	3	2	37
67.	A. Hay	Gladstone A.C., (Canada)	3	3	17
68.	M.C Hawkes	Maidstone H.	3	4	03
69.	G. Neil	Hawkhill H.	3	4	12
70.	J. O'Neil	Radcliffe H.	3	6	23
71.	I. Turnbull	Falkirk Victoria H.	3	8	32
72.	R. Boyd	Clydesdale H.	3	10	39
73.	G.W. Hawkins	Sunningdale A.C.	3	17	38
74.	D.A. Hope	Unattached	3	22	13
75.	I.W. Pratt	Rotherham H.	3	25	44
76.	D. Leviston	Barrow A.C.	3	31	35
	G. Goodair	Wakefield H.	Retired		
	J. Mcinally	Dundee Thistle H.	Retired		
	W. J. Hannan	Barrow A.C.	Retired		
	R. Russell	Belgrave H.	Retired		
	A. Milton	Pitreavie A.C.	Retired		
	J. Petrie	Dundee Thistle H.	Retired		

Team Places

			Points
1.	Lochaber A.C. "A"	(4-5-16)	25
2.	Pitreavie A.C.	(12-13-27)	52
3.	Springburn H.	(7-8-45)	60
4.	Lochaber "B".	(20-25-43)	88
5.	Cambuslang H.	(21-26-46)	93
6.	Bellahouston H.	(18-32-49)	99
7.	Wakefield H	(6-40-59)	105
8.	Rotherham"A"	(29-33-51)	113
9.	Springburn H. "B"	(24-42-50)	116
10.	Barrow A.C.	(1-48-76)	125
11.	Vauxhall Motors A.C.	(36-47-60)	143

Race was run in a thunderstorm despite threats of cancellation by some officials.

1959
Saturday 5th September at 2.30pm from King George V Park
Race Starter - Mr Malcolm McCulloch, C.B.E. D.L. (Chief Constable, City of Glasgow Police).

			Hrs	*Mins*	*Secs*
1.	**D.A. Spencer**	**Barrow A.C.**	1	47	53
2.	J. Linaker	Pitreavie (1st Newcomer & Visitor)	1	51	33
3.	F. Dawson	Salford H. & A.C.	1	52	
4.	R. Shaw	Border H.	1	53	47
5.	J. Conn	Lochaber A.C. (1st Local)	1	54	59
6.	D. M. Turner	Liverpool H. & A.C.	1	55	24
7.	W. Lawrence	Forres H.	1	55	26
8.	R. Hill	Clayton-le-Moors	1	55	33
9.	D. Pearson	Leeds Athletic	1	56	47
10.	C. Foley	Pitreavie A.A.C.	1	56	53
11.	H. K. Mitchell	Shettleston H.	1	57	9
12.	A.G. Nowell	Thames Valley H. & R.A.P.	1	58	33
13.	E. Campbell	Lochaber A.C.	1	59	7
14.	A. Heaton	Clayton-le-Moors	1	59	52
15.	M. Vickers	Barrow A.C.	2	1	41
16.	A. Byers	Border H.	2	1	57
17.	I. Donald	Shettleston H.	2	3	3
18.	G. Goodair	Wakefield H. & A.C.	2	3	51
19.	M. Boylen	Vauxhall Motors A.C.	2	5	21
20.	A. Patten	Clayton-le-Moors	2	5	33
21.	K. Heaton	Clayton-le-Moors	2	5	34
22.	G. Bradshaw	Blackpool & Fyide	2	5	52
23.	J. Garvey	Vale of Leven A.A.C.	2	6	55
24.	W. Lindsay	Pitreavie A.A.C.	2	7	15
25.	W. Jamieson	Plebian H.	2	7	30
26.	J. Kerr	Airdrie H.	2	7	47
27.	J. Hand	Border H.	2	8	57
28.	A. Johnstone	Clayton-le-Moors	2	10	17
29.	T. Robertson	Inverness H.	2	11	12
30.	M. Moan	Lochaber A.C.	2	12	38
31.	M. Cameron	Kinlochleven A.C.	2	12	48
32.	A. Bonnor	Maidstone H.	2	12	52
33.	G. Brass	Clayton-le-Moors	2	13	42
34.	J. Bushby	Clayton-le-Moors	2	14	7
35.	P. Boxley	Tipton H.	2	14	24
36.	R. Walker	Wakefield H. & A.C.	2	14	52
37.	H. Soper	Vauxhall Motors A.C.	2	17	33
38.	E. Silk	Tipton H.	2	17	54
39.	J. Brotherhood	United Hospitals Hare & Hounds	2	18	36
40.	R. Poultney	Tipton H.	2	18	45
41.	J. Jacobs	Springburn Harriers	2	18	57
42.	R. Wilson	Bellahouston H.	2	19	38
43.	S. Bradshaw	Clayton-le-Moors (1st Veteran)	2	19	55
44.	G. Douglas	Wakefield H & A.C.	2	20	27
45.	J. Welshman	Pitreavie A.A.C.	2	22	17
46.	D. Thomson	Lochaber A.C.	2	22	22
47.	I. Grainger	Edinburgh Southern H.	2	22	38
48.	K. Clark	Airedale H.	2	25	24
49.	J. Geddes	Monkland H.	2	25	29
50.	W. Charnley	Clayton-le-Moors	2	26	20
51.	D. Watt	Unattached	2	26	51

No.	Name	Club			
52.	T. Mercer	R.N.A.S., Abbotsinch	2	27	0
53.	K. Mitchell	Doncaster Plant Works	2	27	8
54.	F. Kielty	Clydesdale H.	2	28	50
55.	I. Campbell	Falkirk Victoria H.	2	29	26
56.	A. Layton	Vauxhall Motors A.C.	2	31	49
57.	D Large	Barrow A.C.	2	32	46
58.	M. Stag	Unattached	2	32	47
59.	P. Littlewood	United Hospitals Hare & Hounds	2	33	19
60.	E. Vine	Maidstone H.	2	34	15
61.	H. Cameron	Lochaber A.C.	2	35	42
62.	P. Moore	Barrow A.C.	2	38	10
63.	R. Lewis	Unattached	2	38	31
64.	J. MacEachern	Shettleston H.	2	40	20
65.	A. Fern	Tipton H.	2	40	24
66.	D. Barker	Leeds Harehills H. & A.C.	2	40	46
67.	R. Boyd	Clydesdale H.	2	44	4
68.	A. Hume	Lochaber A.C.	2	45	5
69.	M. Hawkes	Maidstone H.	2	47	2
70.	P. Bull	Ranleigh H.	2	47	13
71.	R. Evans	Darlington H.	2	49	37
72.	C. Bulpitt	Andvoor & Dist A.C.	2	49	55
73.	A. Winter	Ranleigh H.	2	51	29
74.	A. Milton	Pitreavie A.C.	2	53	21
75.	J. Campbell	Lochaber A.C	2	53	50
76.	F. Palmer	Barrow A.C.	2	55	59
77.	G. Seabrook	Vauxhall Motors A.C.	2	58	22
78.	R. Walker	Unattached	2	59	54
79.	H. Lofts	R.N.A.S., Abbotsinch	3	0	50
80.	R. Puckrin	Middlesborough & Cleveland H.	3	4	57
81.	G. Charnley	Lunesdale A.C.	3	6	9
82.	J. Slocket	Clayton-le-Moors	3	8	23
83.	J. Hume	R.A.F.	3	10	29
84.	D. McQueen	Shettleston H.	3	13	29
85.	R. Lawson	Clayton-le-Moors	3	15	17
86.	D. Williamson	Pitreavie A.A.C.	3	19	51
87.	D. Aldred	South London H. & R.A.F.	3	36	24
88.	G. Neil	Dundee Hawkhill H.	3	40	5
	B. Smethurst	Plebian H.	Retired		
	A. Edwards	Abbotsinch A.C.	Retired		
	R. Thorpe	Tipton H.	Retired		
	W. Hunter	Lochaber A.C.	Retired		
	E. Robb	Unattached	Retired		
	T. Bower	Pitreavie A.C.	Retired		

Team Places			**Points**
1.	Pitreavie 'A'	(2-10-24)	36
2.	Clayton-le-Moors 'A'	(8-14-21)	43
3.	Border Harriers	(4-16-27)	47
4.	Lochaber Athletic 'A'	(5-13-30)	48
5.	Barrow Athletic	(1-15-57)	73
6.	Clayton-le-Moors 'B'	(20-34-43)	97
7.	Vauxhall Motors	(19-37-56)	112
8.	Tipton Harriers	(35-38-40)	113
9.	Maidstone Harriers	(32-60-69)	161

Trophies and medals were inscribed before the presentation which was conducted by Dick MacTaggart, Olympic boxing champion.

1960
Saturday 4th September at 2.30pm from King George V Park
Race Starter - Mr J. W. Hobbs

			Hrs	Mins	Secs
1.	**D.A. Spencer**	**Barrow**	**1**	**52**	**22**
2.	M. Vickers	Barrow (lst Visitor)	1	52	23
3.	J. Conn	Lochaber (lst Local)	1	54	8
4.	J. Severen	Tipton (lst Newcomer)	1	54	45
5.	F. Dawson	Salford H.	1	54	58
6.	E. Campbell	Lochaber	1	55	19
7.	M. Cameron	Lochaber	1	55	38
8.	T. O'Reilly	Springburn	1	56	3
9.	M. Logie	Springburn	1	56	58
10.	G. Garnet	Bingley	1	57	23
11.	B. Smith	Hamilton Olympia (Canada)	1	57	52
12.	H. Bell	Morpeth	1	58	56
13.	D. MacKenzie	Clydesdale	2	0	32
14.	G. Barrow	Preston	2	0	44
15.	G. Goodair	Wakefield	2	1	17
16.	P. Hall	Barrow	2	2	7
17.	E. Holmes	Burn Road	2	2	50
18.	S. Wilkie	Gateshead	2	3	5
19.	D. Bell	Liverpool	2	3	16
20.	G. Bradshaw	Blackpool & Fylde	2	4	0
21.	M. Boylen	Vauxhall Motors	2	4	31
22.	C. P. Grundie	Salford	2	5	18
23.	M. Moore	H.M.S. Caledonia	2	6	5
24.	A. Norrie	Kinlochleven	2	6	37
25.	H. Soper	Vauxhall Motors	2	6	58
26.	W. A. R. Lindsay	Pitreavie	2	7	18
27.	A. Paton	Clayton-le-Moors	2	7	32
28.	P. Duffy	Aberdeen	2	7	45
29.	I. Donald	Shettleston	2	7	48
30.	N. Chisholm	Lochaber	2	7	59
31.	A. B. Westwood	Dudley	2	8	10
32.	R. Duncan	Aberdeen	2	8	59
33.	K. Heaton	Clayton-le-Moors	2	10	23
34.	A. J. Whittle	Tipton	2	11	16
35.	R. Poultney	Tipton	2	11	16
36.	M. Moan	Lochaber	2	11	19
37.	B. Hatch	Lochaber	2	12	58
38.	A. Bonner	Maidstone	2	13	34
39.	A. Johnstone	Clayton-le-Moors	2	14	4
40.	C. Lawson		2	14	7
41.	E. Silk	Tipton	2	14	30
42.	D.L. Anderson	Bingley	2	14	49
43.	C. Greenlees	Perth	2	15	29
44.	R. Craven	Bingley	2	16	17
45.	J. Shackley	Barrow	2	16	50
46.	C.W. Foley	Pitreavie	2	17	14
47.	T.R. Puckrin	Middlesborough	2	17	59
48.	R. Wilson	Bellahouston	2	18	52
49.	J. Slocket	Clayton-le-Moors	2	20	6
50.	S. Bradshaw	Clayton-le-Moors (lst Veteran)	2	20	47
51.	A. Layton	Vauxhall Motors	2	22	1
52.	I. Morrison	Aberdeen	2	23	14
53.	A. Morrison	Lochaber	2	23	29
54.	D. Large	Barrow	2	25	29
55.	J. G. Day	Dudley	2	25	34

56.	J. Geddes	Monkland	2	25	35
57.	R. J. Barrett	Pitreavie	2	25	35
58.	H. Simpson	Barrow	2	25	43
59.	A. Lewis	United Hospitals	2	25	50
60.	K. Cox	Jun. Mountaineering Club of Scot.	2	26	52
61.	D. Lawson	Bingley	2	26	54
62.	B. Cook	Unattached	2	28	5
63.	R. Lewney	Barrow	2	28	50
64.	B. Goodfellow	Pitreavie	2	29	12
65.	D. Bowman	Clydesdale	2	29	32
66.	W. J. Hannan	Barrow	2	29	58
67.	C/fn. Gill	R.A. Training Regt.	2	34	39
68.	J. Armstrong	Dudley	2	34	58
69.	W. Mcintyre	Monkland	2	35	52
70.	J. Betney	Sefton	2	36	21
71.	E. Slaughter	Morpeth	2	36	40
72.	G. Charnley	Clayton-le-Moors	2	37	8
73.	R. West	Middlesborough	2	37	10
74.	M.C. Hawkes	Maidstone	2	38	33
75.	D. Thomson	Lochaber	2	39	48
76.	I. D. Gow	Inverness	2	40	40
77.	T. J. Cox	R.A.F. Waddington	2	40	44
78.	Gnr. Malpass	R.A. Training Regt.	2	41	29
79.	J.M. Cartwright	Weymouth	2	41	41
80.	A. Fleming	Cambuslang	2	42	34
81.	C. Laing	Inverness	2	43	19
82.	J.S. Hume	Unattached	2	43	27
83.	R. Evans	Darlington	2	43	34
84.	R. Boyd	Clydesdale	2	48	57
85.	E.J. Vine	Maidstone	2	50	36
86.	J. MacEachern	Shettleston	2	52	52
87.	D. Edwards	Unattached	2	53	17
88.	M. MacFarlane	Unattached	2	53	23
89.	G. Seabrook	Vauxhall Motors	2	54	50
90.	R. Hill	Clayton-le-Moors	2	56	57
91.	A. Rowley	Unattached	2	57	56
92.	J. Haydon	Dudley	2	58	8
93.	G. Neil	Dundee	3	2	25
94.	J. M. Stewart	Clydesdale	3	3	56
95.	G. Wilson	Unattached	3	6	9
96.	L. Hutchison	Springburn	3	8	14
97.	N. Moon	Maidstone	3	38	0

Team Positions   **Points**

1.	Lochaber A.C. "A"	(3-6-7)	16
2.	Barrow A.C. "A"	(1-2-16)	19
3.	Tipton Harriers	(4-34-35)	73
4.	Bingley Harriers	(10-42-44)	96
5.	Vauxhall Motors A.C.	(21-25-51)	97
6.	Clayton-le-Moors"A"	(27-33-39)	99
7.	Aberdeen A.A.C.	(28-32-52)	112
8.	Springburn Harriers	(8-9-96)	113
9.	Lochaber A.C. "B"	(30-37-53)	120
10.	Pitreavie A.C.	(26-46-57)	129
11.	Dudley Harriers	(31-55-68)	154
12.	Barrow A.C. "B"	(45-54-58)	157
13.	Clydesdale Harriers	(13-65-84)	162
14.	Clayton-le-Moors"B"	(49-50-72)	171
15.	Maidstone Harriers	(38-74-85)	197

97 runners finish the course, the best yet. A Canadian comes within five and a half minutes of winning. Lochaber win back the team trophy.

The Ben Race 1994

Main Results

<table>
<tr><td colspan="2">CATEGORY ABBREVIATIONS</td></tr>
</table>

CATEGORY ABBREVIATIONS
A - Lochaber District Resident; **B** - Under 23 Years of Age; **C** - Over 40 Years of Age(Ladies over 35); **D** - Over 50 Years of Age (Ladies over 45); **E** - First Ben Nevis Race; **F** - 21st Ben Nevis Race; **G** - Serving in H M Forces; **H** - Serving in Police; **I** - Serving in Fire Brigade; **J** - Lady

1	01:30:17	**38** HOLMES, Ian	**Bingley Harriers & AC**	
2	01:31:06	**66** BLAND, Gavin	Borrowdale Fell Runners	B
3	01:31:33	**67** BLAND, Jonathon	Borrowdale Fell Runners	B
4	01:33:12	**274** RODGERS, Billy	Lochaber AC	AG
5	01:34:41	**339** SHEARD, Paul	Pudsey & Bramley AC	
6	01:35:03	**10** JAMIESON, Robin	Ambleside AC	
7	01:35:44	**207** JACKSON, Steve	Horwich RMI Harriers	C
8	01:36:03	**52** WHITFIELD, Bob	Bingley Harriers & AC	C
9	01:36:22	**148** BOWNESS, Alan	Cumberland Fell Runners	
10	01:36:39	**183** BARTLETT, Graeme	Forres Harriers	
11	01:39:06	**192** MARSHALL, Brian	Haddington E Lothian Pacers	E
12	01:39:08	**245** BURNS, Stephen	Lochaber AC	AB
13	01:39:12	**335** DEVINE, Gary	Pudsey & Bramley AC	
14	01:39:14	**70** SCHOFIELD, Andrew	Borrowdale Fell Runners	
15	01:39:29	**390** WRENCH, Andrew	Todmorden Harriers	
16	01:39:41	**336** GREEN, Shane	Pudsey & Bramley AC	
17	01:39:53	**116** NUTTALL, Dave	Clayton-le-Moors Harriers	
18	01:40:13	**257** HEPBURN, John	Lochaber AC	A
39	01:40:34	**200** KELMAN, Norman	Highland Hill Runners	
20	01:40:49	**69** HICKS, Stephen G	Borrowdale Fell Runners	
21	01:41:40	**410** BENNET, Sandy	Westerlands Cross Country	
22	01:42:31	**345** JONES, Trefor H	Rhedwyr Eryri Harriers	
23	01:42:49	**238** ANDERSON, Callum	Lochaber AC	A
24	01:43:06	**43** MITCHELL, Paul	Bingley Harriers & AC	
25	01:43:11	**55** LANAGHAN, Nigel	Black Combe Runners	
26	01:43:46	**337** KEMPLEY, Rupert	Pudsey & Bramley AC	E
27	01:43:52	**263** MACRAE, John A	Lochaber AC	A
28	01:44:38	**49** THORNBER, Andrew	Bingley Harriers & AC	
29	01:45:23	**105** HOLT, Jack	Clayton-le-Moors Harriers	C
30	01:55:41	**134** SHIELDS, James	Clydesdale Harriers	C
31	01:45:55	**127** THOMPSON, Lee	Clayton-le-Moors Harriers	
32	01:46:17	**209** WALTON, Brian	Horwich RMI Harriers	C
33	01:46:39	**64** MARTIN, Paul	Bolton United Harriers	
34	01.47.15	**140** KAMMER, Philip	Cosmic Hillbashers	
35	01:47:25	**40** JEBB, Robert	Bingley Harriers & AC	B
36	01:47:44	**391** WRIGHT, Jonathan	Todmorden Harriers	E

37	01:47:49	330 WHITTET, Jeremy	Perth Strathtay Harriers	
38	01:47:58	340 STEVENSON, Brian	Pudsey & Bramley AC	
39	01:48:01	251 CRAIG, Andrew	Lochaber AC	A
40	01:48:27	73 SHEARD, James Herbert	Calder Valley Fell Runners	C
41	01:48.32	96 CARR, Kieran	Clayton-le-Moors Harriers	C
42	01:48:54	282 SMITH, Ian Cameron	Lochaber AC	AE
43	01:49:34	387 SCHOFIELD, B	Todmorden Harriers	CE
44	01 49:45	303 PEARSON, David	Mandale Harriers & AC	E
45	01.49:59	117 NUTTALL, John	Clayton-le-Moors Harriers	CD
46	01:50:01	53 WILKINSON, Chris	Bingley Harriers & AC	C
47	01:50:05	243 BROOKS, Graham	Lochaber AC	AC
48	01:50:50	242 BROOKS, Billy	Lochaber AC	AC
49	01:50:52	264 MAITLAND, John R	Lochaber AC	A
50	01:51:07	56 SMITH, Peter Graham	Black Combe Runners	E
51	01:51:14	11 PARKER, Eric David	Ambleside AC	C
52	01:51:47	80 FLYNN, Martin	Carnethy Hill Running	E
53	01:52:55	87 SHIELL, Douglas	Carnethy Hill Running	
54	01:53:03	327 SMITH, Anthony Peter	Pennine Fell Runners	
55	01:53:06	329 MACKAY, Euan	Perth Strathtay Harriers	E
56	01:53:32	194 ELLIS, Tor	Heriot Watt University AC	BE
57	01:53:36	277 SCOTT, Alastair	Lochaber AC	C
58	01:54:02	143 MACDONALD, Dennis	Cosmic Hillbashers	E
59	01:54:15	354 RAWLINSON, Barry	Rossendale Harriers & AC	C
60	01:54:27	8 BETTNEY, Philip	Ambleside AC	C
61	01:54:41	201 MACDONALD, Iain	Highland Hill Runners	
62	01:54:53	270 NOLAN, Scott (Inverlochy)	Lochaber AC	A
63	01:54:54	141 LAWRIE, Brian	Cosmic Hillbashers	C
64	01:54:59	349 SMITH, Steve	Ripon Runners	C
65	01:55:16	150 PEDEN, Andrew	Cumberland Fell Runners	H
66	01:55:24	260 LANCASTER, Nic	Lochaber AC	C
67	01:55:28	153 HUTTON, Robert	Dark Peak Fell Runners	E
68	01:55:46	174 HOLDEN, Joe	Fife AC	C
69	01:56:04	290 MACLEAN, Donald S	Lomond Hill Runners	
70	01:56:16	320 BUCHANAN, Peter	Ochil Hill Runners	
71	01:56:30	197 BRETT, Alexander	Highland Hill Runners	C
72	01:56:50	383 ASHTON, David	Todmorden Harriers	
73	01:56:55	361 BLAIN, Gordon	Scottish Borders AC	I
74	01:57:22	377 NICHOL, Colin	Teviotdale Harriers	
75	01:57:31	13 WALKER, Norman	Ambleside AC	C
76	01:57:37	157 ASPEY, Stephen	Denbigh Harriers	
77	01:57:40	155 TAYLOR, Gary	Darwen Dashers RC	E
78	01:57:55	115 NIELD, David Leslie	Clayton-le-Moors Harriers	
79	01:58:25	419 WHITE, Kenneth	Westerlands Cross Country	C
80	01:58:26	208 MURRAY, Paul	Horwich RMI Harriers	CDF
81	01:58:56	225 COVELL, Marcus	Kildalton AC	
82	01:58:59	280 SMITH, Brian	Lochaber AC	A
83	01:59:12	287 GRAHAM, Alan	Lomond Hill Runners	C
84	01:59:40	375 MARSH, John Poulson	Teviotdale Harriers	C
85	01:59:44	351 LEE, Andrew	Rochdale Harriers & AC	
86	01:59:46	61 KEARNS, Dennis	Bolton United Harriers	C

87	01:59:53	60 CROOK, Edward	Bolton United Harriers	C
88	01:59:57	328 WYATT, Steven	Pennine Fell Runners	
89	02:00:00	247 CAMPBELL, Ruairidh	Lochaber AC	
90	02:00:02	393 BOLER, Paul	Totley AC	BE
91	02:00:23	406 HORSLEY, Brian	West Yorkshire Fire Service	CI
92	02:00:37	322 STEPHEN, Jack	Ochil Hill Runners	C
93	02:00:39	28 BELL, Douglas	Bingley Harriers & AC	CH
94	02:00:46	109 LEE, Michael Jeffrey	Clayton-le-Moors Harriers	
95	02:00:56	300 DAVIS, Stephen	Mandale Harriers & AC	
96	02:00:58	146 RENNIE, Ewen	Cosmic Hillbashers	C
97	02:01:06	9 HICKS, Michael	Ambleside AC	
98	02:01:19	164 FRASER, Ian	East Cheshire Harriers	E
99	02:01:37	338 SEIPP, Richard	Pudsey & Bramley AC	E
100	02:01:46	107 JUDGE, Francis	Clayton-le-Moors Harriers	C
101	02:02:06	31 DOBSON, Kevin	Bingley Harriers & AC	
102	02:02:11	392 BOLER, Neville	Totley AC	C
103	02 02 16	175 MCGILLIVRAY, Alan	Fife AC	CD
104	02.02.24	161 LOVE, Charlie	Dundee Hawkhill Harriers	CD
105	02:02:33	4 NORMAN, Jeff	Altrincham AC	C
106	02:02:34	99 DUGDALE, Andrew Mark	Clayton-le-Moors Harriers	E
107	02:02:40	190 MCLOONE, Stephen	Greenock Glenpark Harriers	E
108	02:03:01	237 WALKER, Peter	Lancaster & Morecambe AC	E
109	02:03:23	158 HUGHES, Michael	Denbigh Harriers	EH
110	02:03:28	240 BANKS, John	Lochaber AC	AC
111	02:03:31	395 CAVE, Michael J	Tyne & Wear Metropolitan FB	EI
112	02:03:32	235 SLINN, Jim	Lancaster & Morecambe AC	C
113	02:03:42	302 MULROONEY, Ian	Mandale Harriers & AC	
114	02:03:45	255 FORSTER, Damian	Lochaber AC	AE
115	02:03:47	212 GRANT, Donald	Inverness Harriers	
116	02:03:50	326 SCOTTNEY, Richard	Pennine Fell Runners	C
117	02:03:55	36 HARGREAVES, William	Bingley Harriers & AC	CH
118	02:04:07	244 BROWN, Richard	Lochaber AC	C
119	02:04:07	198 BROWN, Philip K	Highland Hill Runners	C
120	02:04:07	176 MCGUIRE, Alex	Fife AC	C
121	02:04:07	59 BELLIS, Peter Alan	Bolton United Harriers	
122	02:04:27	420 BRANNAN, Terence	Whitburn AC	
123	02:04:27	262 MACLENNAN, Alastair	Lochaber AC	A
124	02:04:33	254 FISH, John M	Lochaber AC	AC
125	02:04:34	346 GRIFFITHS, Glyn Alun	Rhedwyr Hebog	
126	02:05:13	389 TALBOT, Joseph	Todmorden Harriers	C
127	02:05.28	79 COX, James,	Carnethy Hill Running	E
128	02:05:36	288 LAMB, James	Lomond Hill Runners	E
129	02:05:42	316 TROUP, Steven	North Shields Polytechnic AC	
130	02:06:12	100 ECCLES, Graham	Clayton-le-Moors Harriers	
131	02:06:17	131 DIVER, Michael	Clydesdale Harriers	E
132	02:06:29	93 BRADY, Martin	Clayton-le-Moors Harriers	
133	02:06:34	222 UNSWORTH, George F	Kendal AC	C
134	02:06:40	29 CALVERT, William John	Bingley Harriers & AC	
135	02:07:05	83 MAIR, James	Carnethy Hill Running	C
136	02:07:16	293 DOWNIE, Chris	Lothian & Borders Police AC	

137	02:07:44	113 MITCHELL, Robert Wilson	Clayton-le-Moors Harriers	C
138	02.07.46	85 PRITCHARD, Colin	Carnethy Hill Running	CD
139	02:07:56	234 OLDROYD, John	Lancaster & Morecambe AC	CE
140	02:08:02	63 KELLY, Mike	Bolton United Harriers	C
141	02:08:28	224 BLENKINSOP, Harry	Keswick AC	CD
142	02:08:33	407 JONES, Allan	West Yorkshire Fire Service	C
143	02:08:36	265 MCALLISTER, Kenny	Lochaber AC	A
144	02:08:41	111 MCCANN, M G	Clayton-le-Moors Harriers	
145	02:08:42	77 NEWELL, Mark	Cambridge Harriers	
146	02:08:43	309 BARR, Andrew William	Mid Argyll AC	
147	02:08:50	404 BUCKLE, Adrian	West Yorkshire Fire Service	EI
148	02:08:56	272 ORR, Ernie	Lochaber AC	ACD
149	02:08:59	167 POLLARD, Robert	Fell Runners Association	E
150	02:09:00	371 BARNFATHER, Ewan	Teviotdale Harriers	E
151	02:09:03	227 CORRIS, Phil	Lancashire Constabulary	CH
152	02:09:06	342 WHITEHEAD, Neil	Pudsey & Bramley AC	
153	02:09:09	213 MACPHERSON, Bryan	Inverness Harriers	A
154	02:09:26	250 CHRYSTAL, Ian	Lochaber AC	ACD
155	02:09:27	355 GEESON, John Nicholas	Ryde Harriers	CD
156	02:10:01	321 CLARKE, Gavin	Ochil Hill Runners	C
157	02:10:12	385 MORRISON, Wayne	Todmorden Harriers	E
158	02:10:27	312 WHYTE, Alexander Duthie	Minolta Black Isle AC	CD
159	02:10:40	72 BRADLEY, Tony	Calder Valley Fell Runners	
160	02.10.45	380 SPENCE, Barry	Teviotdale Harriers	CE
161	02:10:48	308 HALL, Brian A M	Metro Aberdeen RC	C
162	02.11.09	196 AMOUR, Dick	Highland Hill Runners	CD
163	02:11. 20	313 BRAY, Kevin	Morpeth Harriers	H
164	02:11:30	154 COLL, Dominic	Darwen Dashers RC	E
165	02:11:37	147 BELL, Michael	Cumberland Fell Runners	C
166	02:11:40	301 LAING, Andrew	Mandale Harriers & AC	E
167	02:11:43	101 FIRTH, Andrew Peter	Clayton-le-Moors Harriers	
168	02:11:45	364 TINDALE, Steven	South Shields Harriers & AC	E
169	02:11:52	94 BRADY, Peter	Clayton-le-Moors Harriers	
170	02:12:10	177 MEIKLJOHN, A	Fife AC	CE
171	02:12:22	75 PATERSON, Archibald	Calderglen Harriers	C
172	02:12:26	91 CARSON-JONES, Simon	City of Portsmouth AC	BE
173	02:12:38	128 WALMSLEY, Andrew J	Clayton-le-Moors Harriers	C
174	02:13:21	178 MITCHELL, M	Fife AC	E
175	**02:13:22**	**241 BARNES, Gill**	**Lochaber AC**	**ACEJ**
176	02:13:27	248 CANT, Robert	Lochaber AC	AC
177	02:13:32	119 RAWLINSON, Jean	Clayton-le-Moors Harriers	CJ
178	02:13:32	165 FULTON, Roy Shields	East Kilbride AC	CI
179	02:13:50	233 HOLDEN, Graham David	Lancaster & Morecambe AC	
180	02:14:04	122 ROGAN, Paul	Clayton-le-Moors Harriers	C
181	02:14:30	283 WALKER, Dave	Lochaber AC	AC
182	02:14:38	394 BOYLE, Tim	Totley AC	CE
183	02:14:43	299 NEWMAN, Dave	Loughton AC	
184	02:14:44	405 BURROWS, Robert	West Yorkshire Fire Service	EI
185	02:15:14	298 MAYCRAFT, Anthony	Loughton AC	E
186	02:15:27	137 CHAPMAN, S	Cosmic Hillbashers	E

187	02:15:38	21 FARQUHARSON, David R	Arbroath Footers	
188	02:15:49	1 ALLEN, RF	Aberdeen AC	
189	02:15:59	368 WAKE, Adrian Paul	Strathearn Harriers	C
190	02:15:59	125 SMITH, John	Clayton-le-Moors Harriers	CD
191	02:16:40	396 ARMSTRONG, David	Tynedale Harriers	E
192	02:16:44	343 EVANS, Gary R	Rhedwyr Eryri Harriers	
193	02:16:57	54 CLARKE, Andrew	Black Combe Runners	E
194	02:17:15	325 MORIARTY, Carl	Pennine Fell Runners	
195	02:17:21	315 RICHARDSON, Colin	North Shields Polytechnic AC	CH
196	02:17:47	261 MACLEAN, A	Lochaber AC	A
197	02:17:53	15 JENVEY, Christopher P	Andover HSA AC	E
198	02:17:58	203 LAVERICK, Keith J	Horsforth Fellandale	E
199	02:18:16	239 ANDERSON, Julie	Lochaber AC	ABJ
200	02:18:18	173 GREIG, Gordon E	Fife AC	C
201	02:18:23	397 FLETCHER, Ruth	Tynedale Harriers	CJ
202	02:18:29	126 THOMPSON, Harry	Clayton-le-Moors Harriers	CD
203	02:18:31	284 WILLIAMS, David Noel	Lochaber AC	AC
204	02:19:01	268 MCINNES, Kevin	Lochaber AC	E
205	02:19:48	399 MCGROGAN, Bill	Valley Striders	C
206	02:19:54	159 BILTCLIFFE, Alan L	Dundee Hawkhill Harriers	C
207	02:19:57	217 HOLDEN, William Lindsay	Jn Greig Builders Central AC	C
208	02:20:35	142 MARKS Graeme	Cosmic Hillbashers	CE
209	02:21:06	37 HALBREY, Andrew	Bingley Harriers & AC	C
210	02:21:28	408 RUSHWORTH, Michael	West Yorkshire Fire Service	EI
211	02:21:29	286 GATEHOUSE, Richard	Lomond Hill Runners	C
212	02:21:31	253 DOUGAN, John Robertson	Lochaber AC	AC
213	02:21:37	182 YORK, Andrew	Forfar Road Runners	
214	02:21:41	180 WEST, Nicholas	FMC Carnegie Harriers	C
215	02:21:43	226 BROADBENT, Steven	Lancashire Constabulary	H
216	02:21:47	350 THACKWRAY, Terry	Ripon Runners	CE
217	02:21:55	17 KINNEAR, William	Annan & District AC	C
218	02:22:02	34 FORD, Michael	Bingley Harriers & AC	C
219	02:22:10	170 WALKER, Frank	Fell Runners Association	CD
220	02:22:33	179 WEST, Alison	FMC Carnegie Harriers	CJ
221	02:22:40	376 MITCHELL, Robert	Teviotdale Harriers	CD
222	02:22:58	332 HACK, Chris	Portsmouth Joggers	CE
223	02:23:18	366 KIRKDALE, Brian G	Steyning AC	G
224	02:23:20	333 YETTON, David	Portsmouth Joggers	C
225	02:23:30	331 CHANNING, Paul	Portsmouth Joggers	
226	02:23:34	356 LEAL, Andy	Ryde Harriers	
227	02:23:41	88 MILNER, David	Chapel Allerton Road Runners E	
228	02:23:56	171 BUCHAN, Peter	Fife AC	E
229	02:23:56	398 SCORER, Chris	Tynedale Harriers	C
230	02:23:59	319 ROBINSON, Mick	Notts AC	
231	02:24:04	76 STEWART, James	Calderglen Harriers	C
232	02:24:10	230 DOYLE, J F	Lancaster & Morecambe AC	C
233	02:24:14	188 STEWART, Ercus	Glenasmole AC (Ireland)	
234	02:24:14	228 HORNE, Michael	Lancashire Constabulary	DJ
235	02:24:27	166 TURNBULL, Drew	East Kilbride AC	CD
236	02:24:38	367 SIDEBOTTOM, Eric William	Strathearn Harriers	CD

237	02:24:44	95 BROWN, Derrick	Clayton-le-Moors Harriers	CD
238	02:24:53	292 CAMPBELL, Ian	Lothian & Borders Police AC	CH
239	02:25:20	25 ATKINSON, Harry	Bingley Harriers & AC	C
240	02:26:10	89 TEMPLE, Graham	Chapel Allerton Road Runners	CE
241	02:26:23	294 HUNTER, Bill	Lothian & Borders Police AC	H
242	02:26:27	415 OSMOND, Christopher	Westerlands Cross Country	C
243	02:26:29	14 WALMSLEY, Neil J	Ambleside AC	C
244	02:26:31	112 MITCHELL, Anthony Ian	Clayton-le-Moors Harriers	CE
245	02:26:53	181 MILNE, Ronald W	Forfar Road Runners	
246	02:27:11	139 JOHNSTON, Andrew	Cosmic Hillbashers	E
247	02:27:12	256 HENDERSON, Nicola	Lochaber AC	AEJ
248	02:27:21	104 HENDERSON, John C	Clayton-le-Moors Harriers	C
249	02:27:40	372 COLTMAN, Alan J	Teviotdale Harriers	
250	02:27:41	215 NICOL, Robert B	Irvine AC	CH
251	02:28:07	384 EDWARDS, Matthew	Todmorden Harriers	E
252	02:28:11	379 PRINGLE, Bill	Teviotdale Harriers	CD
253	02:28:19	304 SYMONDS, Trevor	Mandale Harriers & AC	E
254	02:28:26	400 COLEMAN, Peter	Vauxhall Motors RC	CD
255	02:28:30	421 MCDONALD, Michael F	Wigan & District Harriers AC	CDE
256	02:28:40	231 HAYLER, Mark	Lancaster & Morecambe AC	C
257	02:28:46	413 GORMAN, Richard M	Westerlands Cross Country	CD
258	02:29:06	102 GEE, Frank	Clayton-le-Moors Harriers	C
259	02:29:10	120 RICHARDSON, Kenneth	Clayton-le-Moors Harriers	CDE
260	02:29:22	314 HAYES, Ray	Morpeth Harriers	CD
261	02:29:23	318 ROBINSON, Peter	Northern Veterans AC	CD
262	02:29:40	334 EVANS, Brian	Prestatyn AC	CD
263	02:29:53	220 RUSHTON, Colin Leslie	Kendal AC	CD
264	02:29:55	285 BEVERIDGE, Bob	Lomond Hill Runners	CD
265	02:30:19	418 STRUTHERS, Ian	Westerlands Cross Country	
266	02:30:S9	78 BROWN, Eric C	Carnethy Hill Running	CE
267	02:30:59	279 SLATER, Sandy	Lochaber AC	A
268	02:31:42	168 PRICE, Ken	Fell Runners Association	C
269	02:31:45	296 CASH, Frederick John	Loughton AC	CD
270	02:32:10	16 BUCHANAN, Jim	Annan & District AC	CD
271	02:32:14	114 MOORE, Edward A	Clayton-le-Moors Harriers	
272	02:32:43	18 BENHAM, Frank	Arbroath Footers	CD
273	02:32:48	172 CATION, Frank William	Fife AC	C
274	02:32:57	378 PITTILLO, Jim	Teviotdale Harriers	CDE
275	02:33:21	216 DRUMMOND, Jim	Jn Greig Builders Central AC C	
276	02:33:28	202 TAIT, R	Hinckley MC	CE
277	02:33:33	24 COSTELLO, Robert	Army AA	CG
278	02:33:40	259 JARDINE, Jimmy	Lochaber AC	CI
279	02:33:42	218 GRESTY, John Keith	Kendal AC	CDE
280	02:33:56	258 HOPE, Lesley	Lochaber AC	CJ
281	02:33:56	412 GORMAN, Manuel	Westerlands Cross Country	
282	02:33:88	27 BEANLAND, Richard	Bingley Harriers & AC	E
283	02:34:17	324 BENNET, W E (Bill)	Penicuik Harriers	CD
284	02:34:45	211 FOGGO, Kenneth	Inverness Harriers	A
285	02:35:12	269 MITCHELL, Stewart	Lochaber AC	AC
286	02:35:44	363 JEROME, N P	Silson Joggers AC	CE

287	02:35:58	129 WHALLEY, Neil	Clayton-le-Moors Harriers	C
288	02:36:06	82 MACKINTOSH, William	Carnethy Hill Running	C
289	02:37:38	74 BEGG, Alister	Calderglen Harriers	C
290	02:38:37	20 CLARK, Isobel	Arbroath Footers	CDJ
291	02:40:37	409 TROTH, Robert	West Yorkshire Fire Service	CI
292	02:41:17	30 DOBSON, Frank	Bingley Harriers & AC	C
293	02:41:42	306 SHORT, Alan John	Meltham Zero AC	C
294	02:41:44	386 NEWBY, John	Todmorden Harriers	CD
295	02:42:17	246 CAMPBELL, Edward	Lochaber AC	ACD
296	02:42:42	138 GREENWOOD, W J	Cosmic Hillbashers	C
297	02:43:10	281 SMITH, Ian	Lochaber AC	AC
298	02:43:22	163 ARMOUR, Allan	East Cheshire Harriers	CE
299	02:43:47	411 BENNY, Graham	Westerlands Cross Country	C
300	02:43:49	360 TOPHAM, Stephen	Saltwell Harriers	CE
301	02:43:56	136 SMALL, Marjorie	Clydesdale Harriers	CDJ
302	02:44:28	271 O'CONNOR, Tommy	Lochaber AC	AC
303	02:46:53	169 SAUNDERS, Mick	Fell Runners Association	E
304	02:47:04	86 ROYLES, Rodney	Carnethy Hill Running	CD
305	02:47:22	323 PRITCHARD, John	Old Sarum Striders	CH
306	02:47:58	145 PRYOR, Steve	Cosmic Hillbashers	E
307	02:48:21	62 KELLY, Annette	Bolton United Harriers	CDJ
308	02:49:22	23 YARNELL, Geoff	Arbroath Footers	C
309	02:51:08	22 WILKINS, John James	Arbroath Footers	CD
310	02:53:53	71 MACDONALD, Bill	Bruce Triathlon	C
311	02:54:52	229 BAKER, Reginald	Lancaster & Morecambe AC	CD
312	02:57:44	370 READE, Jon	Telford AC	E
313	02:58:35	186 FOGARTY, Hank	Glenasmole AC (Ireland)	CDE
314	02:58:42	92 ASHWORTH, Kieron David	Clayton-le-Moors Harriers	E
315	03:01:45	132 KING, Shelagh Ann	Clydesdale Harriers	CJ
316	03:01:58	195 ALLEMANO, Ralph	Highgate Harriers	C
317	03:02:19	365 GASTON, Paul	Steyning AC	C
318	03:02:33	214 YOUNG, Henry Swan	Inverness Harriers	CDF
319	03:02:47	106 HUGHES, Peter	Clayton-le-Moors Harriers	
320	03:03:30	403 WARD, Leslie H	Wesham Road Runners	CDE
321	03:03:55	266 MCALLISTER, William Hill	Lochaber AC	ACD
322	03:06:08	388 SMITH, James	Todmorden Harriers	CD
323	03:07:05	124 SHONE, Monica L	Clayton-le-Moors Harriers	CDJ
324	03:09:09	317 HARTLEY, Harry	Northern Veterans AC	CD
325	03:10:00	185 CORRIGAN, Cormac	Glenasmole AC (Ireland)	E
326	03:20:39	401 SOPER, Hugo Albert	Vauxhall Motors RC	CD
327	03:20:39	6 WRIGHT, Arthur	Altrincham AC	CD
328	03:29:27	249 CHISHOLM, Nigel	Lochaber AC	AC

Ben Nevis *Cailean MacLean*

BIBLIOGRAPHY

"There can be no greater enjoyment to the inquisitive mind than to find where he has hitherto found nothing but darkness. More than once I have experienced this agreeable sensation in the process of the current investigation, and I may venture with the more confidence to deliver this Work from my hands to the reader, because happily I can assert, that much which formely appeared to him in doubtful and obscure gloom, will now be seen in the full and clear light of day."

Wiliam F. Skene: *History of the Highlanders of Scotland.*

This bibliography represents a comprehensive list of the main sources used in researching the history of the Ben Race. It is by no means a complete record of all the material ever written about Ben Nevis, only a guide to some of what is available.

Information has also been included on sources which are useful in pursuance of material on other related matters such as Highland history, and specifically the history of the Lochaber area

Sources have been detailed by author where applicable (surname first) and first word of title where no individual author available.

Adomnan, Abbot, *Life of St Columba*, ed. A & O Anderson. London, 1961

Bartlett, Phil, *The Undiscovered Country*. The reason we climb. The Ernest Press, 1993

Barron, Hugh (ed), *The Third Statistical Account of Scotland*. Vol XVI. The County of Inverness. Edinburgh, 1985

Barron, James, *The Northern Highlands in the 19th century*. Three volumes. 1800-1856. Inverness, 1913

Cameron, Walter, *The Burgh of Fort William*. Fort William, 1975

Campbell, Eddie, *Ben Nevis Races, 1951-60, Ten Years*. n.d.

Campbell, J.F., Popular tales of *The West Highlands*. 1861

Drummond-Norie, W., *Loyal Lochaber*. 1898

Duff, David (Ed), *Queen Victoria's Highland Journals*. London, 1980

Gardner, Arthur, *The Peaks, Lochs & Coasts of the Western Highlands*. Edinburgh, 1928

Grant, Isabel, F., *Highland Folk Ways*. 1961

Hunter, James, *Scottish Highlanders*. A People and their Places. Edinburgh and London, 1992

Hunter, James, *A Dance Called America*. Edinburgh, 1994

Hunter, James and MacLean, Cailean, *Skye: The Island*. Edinburgh, 1986

Huyshe, Wentworth *The Life of Saint Columba by Saint Adamnan*. London, 1914

Kilgour, William T., *Twenty Years on Ben Nevis*. Fort William, 1905. (Re-printed 1985, Anglesey Books, Gwynned, Wales.)

Kilgour, William T., *Lochaber in War and Peace*. 1908

MacDonald, Colin M., (ed) *The Third Statistical Account of Scotland*. Vol. IX. The County of Argyll. Edinburgh, 1961

MacDonald, Stuart, *Back to Lochaber*. Edinburgh, 1994

MacGregor, Edith, *The Story of the Fort of Fort William*. 1954

MacKay, John G., *Life in The Highlands a Hundred Years Ago*. (Address to The Gaelic Society of Glasgow) 1890

MacKellar, Mary. *MacDougall's Guide to Lochaber*. 1881

MacLean, Calum, *The Highlands*, Edinburgh, 1990

MacLennan, Hugh D., *An Gearasdan. The First One Hundred Years of Fort William Shinty Club*. Inverness, 1994

MacPhee, G. Graham, Ben Nevis: *Scottish Mountaineering Club Guide*, Edinburgh, 1936

MacPherson, Angus, *A Highlander looks back*. Oban, no date

Mather, Alexander S. (ed), *The Third Statistical Account of Scotland*. Vol XIII. The County of Ross and Cromarty. Edinburgh, 1987

Nature Conservancy Council, *Ben Nevis and Glen Nevis: Wildlife and Geology*. Inverness, 1989

Prebble, John, *The Lion in the North*. London, 1971

Sage, Rev. Donald, *Memorabilia Domestica*. 1899

Somers, Robert, *Letters from the Highlands on the Famine of 1846*. Glasgow, 1848

Steel, Charles W. S., *The Ben Nevis Race*. 1956 and 1959

Stewart, Rev Alexander. *Nether Lochaber*. 1883

Stewart, Rev Alexander. '*Twixt Ben Nevis and Glencoe*'. 1885

The Scottish Mountaineering Club Guides - *The Western Highlands. Ben Nevis. The Central Highlands*.

Thomas, John. T*he West Highland Railway*. 1992

Thomson, Derick, (ed), *The Companion to Gaelic Scotland*. Oxford, 1983